The Reverb series looks at the connections between music, artists and performers, musical cultures and places. It explores how our cultural and historical understanding of times and places may help us to appreciate a wide variety of music, and vice versa.

reverb-series.co.uk
Series editor: John Scanlan

HEROES

DAVID BOWIE AND BERLIN

TOBIAS RÜTHER

REAKTION BOOKS

Published by Reaktion Books Ltd
33 Great Sutton Street
London EC1V 0DX, UK
www.reaktionbooks.co.uk

This is a revised and enlarged edition of Tobias Rüther's *Helden: David Bowie und Berlin*, copyright © Rogner & Bernhard GmbH & Co., Verlags KG, Berlin 2008

First published in English 2014

Translated by Anthony Mathews

English translation and 'Coda' copyright © Reaktion Books 2014

Printed and bound in Great Britain
by Bell & Bain, Glasgow

A catalogue record for this book is available from the British Library

ISBN 978 1 78023 377 2

CONTENTS

Victoria Station, London, 2 May 1976: Bowie returning to Europe from Los Angeles.

INTRODUCTION

Music comes in the night and says: You are not alone.
But why is there one on his own? Because he is a little hero,
different to all the others.

– Diedrich Diederichsen, 1985

And from right here, says the tour guide, at that time you could
see the Wall.

Some of the young people press themselves up against the
window, straining to get a look out. But they can't see anything.
Oh, yes they can: the blank wall of a building, holding out the
prospect of suddenly seeing the world as he saw it. And even if
it isn't the Wall, since it no longer exists, then at least the city.
And even it is not as he saw it, since you can't do that anyway,
then at least from the same angle as he saw it.

But all you can see from the first-floor window of Hansa
Studios in Berlin is the blank wall of a building.

No sign of his past. The focus of the city has shifted in the
ast 30 years. The Kaisersaal of the nearby Grand Hotel Esplanade,
for instance, was relocated when Potsdamer Platz was built up
again after the Wall came down. It was in the shadow of the old
Potsdamer Platz, as it happens, that in the mid-'70s Bowie came
to play what was to prove the most daring music of his career.
In the very same Hansa Studios, in the very same room, and next
door in the Meistersaal, the master mason's hall, behind a wall
that still exists.

That's where there was a video camera set up, and here in
the control room, now called the Grüner Salon, the Green Room,
there was a monitor relaying everything being filmed to the
mixing desk. The equipment came from the Esplanade, then as

now located not far away from here. Crazy, eh? A studio by the Wall, separated by a wall! The fans laugh. Then they strain to get another look, one last look, before the tour of Hansa Studios moves on. It's nothing. Just the blank wall of a building.

Some 200 metres away, behind this wall, just down Köthener Strasse, just over a piece of waste ground, still derelict after 30 years, then straight across Stresemann Strasse: that's where the Wall stood. Plus an East German watchtower. David Bowie made it into an image. He gave it the title 'Heroes'. It shows two lovers standing by the Wall. It was from here that Bowie could see the man and the woman in the shadow of the watchtower.

It's nothing. Just the blank wall of a building.

'We can be Heroes – just for one day', David Bowie sings. Not a day, six minutes: that's how long the single 'Heroes' lasts, and when it's over, it's like it has never been. That's what pop songs are like. They summon up images that go on reverberating in the space between your ears, nowhere else. They make it possible for a simple tune to let you see walls for a moment, sometimes even to see through them. Strange heroes, pop songs.

It was 1977 when Bowie recorded the album *'Heroes'* in Berlin. To commemorate the event 25 years later, it's already necessary for the photographer from a local paper to put the record cover into the picture when photographing the house Bowie occupied at the time in the Schöneberger Hauptstrasse – to have at least something to remind you of the singer.

Blotted out, built over, flattened to the ground, no sign of his past. Apart from the images he made of the city, most of them black-and-white like on the monitor in Hansa Studios, there is nothing to remind you of David Bowie in Berlin.

Or is there? That's what this book is about.

1 THE MAN WHO CAME IN FROM HELL

The Mercedes 600 had once belonged to the President of Sierra Leone. It's black, its top can be opened up at the rear, and it is waiting for passengers on the seafront in Cannes. Possibly, if you go along with another version of the story, it was also once owned by a murdered Iranian prince, and you never know, hey, it may even have belonged to Adolf Hitler himself, given his particular fondness for reviewing his troops from an open-top Mercedes. Anyway, it's black, and if you turn back a page there's a photo to prove it.

It's a very famous, very unfortunate photo as it shows David Bowie, dressed in jet black and pale with hair dyed blond, standing in the open rear of his Mercedes 600. It's Victoria Station on 2 May 1976, a few weeks later than Cannes. Bowie has just this minute got off the Orient Express on Platform 8. There he is in the photo, greeting his fans with his left arm raised. British press photographers and journalists are also there, obsessed as they are with wanting to know which was Hitler's favourite car and the colour of ss uniforms: black of course, and the tabloids go to town on this. It's true then, the headlines announce the following day, we were right after all: David Bowie, the greatest living pop star, identifies with the Nazis, perhaps he's a closet Nazi.

Perhaps, as he argues later, Bowie was only photographed 'mid-wave', and this raised left arm wasn't meant to be a Hitler salute. The videos that appear on the internet move too rapidly to tell. But it's hard to believe this gesture was only an unfortunate coincidence. In fact, as soon as Bowie got into the jet-black secondhand car on the seafront in Cannes along with Iggy Pop at the end of March in 1976 he was mentioned in the papers over and over again in connection with apparent Nazi incidents. The two of them drive north from the Côte d'Azur in the open-top Mercedes. Passing through Germany via Munich, Düsseldorf and Berlin, as Bowie is touring with his *Station to Station* album. They continue on from Germany in the direction of Scandinavia, where Bowie is appearing in Stockholm and Helsinki. As he had done a few years before, they go on by train to Moscow and then back to the West – with them both ending up being stopped on the border between Russia and Poland. Bowie is found to be carrying Nazi stuff in his suitcase, mainly books. Appealing to the border guards, he claims to be doing research for a musical on Goebbels. And he gets away with it.

But he has protested too much in recent times, claiming not to have meant what he said in his over-the-top outbursts. For example, 'Britain could benefit from a fascist leader.' A fascist leader for Britain, you must be joking? 'I mean fascist in its true sense', Bowie explains, 'not Nazi. After all, fascism is really nationalism. In a sense, it's a very pure form of communism.' Bowie is all for a Führer coming to power, the news agencies report the very same day. Bowie vehemently denies that he ever said that. No, instead he tells another journalist: 'The only way we can speed up the sort of liberalism that's hanging foul in the air at the moment is to speed up the progress of a right-wing, totally dictatorial tyranny and get it over as fast as possible.' Then, to add to this, in Berlin he is photographed by Andrew Kent looking contemplatively at a bust of Hitler and doing a Hitler salute on the waste ground covering the site of the Führer's bunker. That, anyway, is what is being said. The pictorial evidence, however, is never released to the public. Not long afterwards Bowie in a black shirt is seen waving to his fans from the open-top Mercedes. This photo at least is published.

But this doesn't prove anything. All it shows is an extremely susceptible, highly sensitive pop artist who has taken on board a bit too much Nietzsche and cocaine for his own good and is a bit out of his depth. He is feeling his way forward towards the next in a series of images, not as yet knowing exactly where he is heading for this time. He wants to go to Berlin, that's for sure. He arrives there in the summer of 1976 but doesn't stay long. It's an episode in his life that has taken on a mythical character in the life of this city with the Wall, a story that has in the meantime become a subject to be endlessly evoked, related and mythologized in newspaper articles, films and city tours. This move to Berlin by David Bowie doesn't happen straightaway, though. His journey begins in the biggest fancy dress party of them all, in Los Angeles, Hollywood, hell on earth.

Since the beginning of his career in London in the early Sixties Bowie had been trying on all sorts of masks. He is the king of fancy dress, fancying himself in everything he tries on, like the 'natural costume boy', the central character in Thomas Mann's *Confessions of Felix Krull, Confidence Man*. He starts out as a Mod in the mid-Sixties, then switches to being a folk singer. In 1969 he has a smash hit with 'Space Oddity' but it isn't followed up by any brilliant sequel. His persona flits from style to style just like a butterfly: trying on Bob Dylan, Lou Reed, John Lennon for size. Then in 1971 he suddenly takes off, writing two proper hits: 'Life on Mars' and 'Changes'. And eventually coming up the following year with 'Ziggy Stardust'.

An icon, something never heard or seen before: a rock 'n' roll messiah. Playing this role, the king of fancy dress cons his way to the top like no other pop musician before him, to the very top, to the end of the universe even, his creature 'Ziggy Stardust' representing an androgynous Martian of Rock. Suddenly he has an enormous army of adoring fans looking up to him as a messiah, a messiah from another planet. A raging hermaphrodite 'with godgiven ass', as Ziggy, that is, Bowie, describes himself in song. *The Rise and Fall of Ziggy Stardust and the Spiders from Mars* is the title of the accompanying album. It was later called 'The record that killed off the Sixties', the album that dealt a death blow to the collective dream that was the 1960s and replaced it with a dream character worshipped by the masses. From now on, rock reigns supreme over the whole world. Millions of people follow 'Ziggy Stardust' and dress up in the same way. Mass psychosis on platform shoes – with powder and make-up.

Bowie is now ready for America. Now, on the eve of his move there, he has largely achieved the dream he has had since the age of eight: of becoming a British Elvis Presley, an idol, someone larger than life.

At this point the boy from the London suburb of Bromley who used to bunk off school sets foot in the land of Elvis. His 1972 tour of America turns into a triumph. Two conmen soulmates cheer 'Ziggy Stardust' performing on the stage of New York's Carnegie Hall: the celebrated Truman Capote and the fetishist of the superficial, Andy Warhol. Also there is Anthony Perkins, the schizophrenic Norman Bates from Hitchcock's *Psycho*. Bowie, half-man, half-woman, the total Alien, has indeed turned into a new Elvis. A naked girl breaks into his apartment and kisses his feet; he sells millions of records around the world. Unlike Elvis, however, success makes him not fatter but skinnier. America means for Bowie a gradual wasting away.

But for the moment, in his rise into the heights in the footsteps of Presley, he is off into orbit in the direction of more remote and inaccessible regions of outer space. His first tour of America is followed by a world tour, and finally in 1974, at the same time as his resettlement in America, by a megalomaniac feat of endurance, the *Diamond Dogs* tour. Fifty elaborately staged concerts, the like of which has never been seen before. The stage sets cost a fortune, there's a movable bridge and even a hydraulic crane. The list of additional props reads like something from a nightmare dreamed up by Giorgio Agamben or George Orwell: it's the world as a prison camp. 'Tanks, turbines, smokestacks', David Bowie wants 'fluorescent lighting, alleyways, cages, watchtowers, girders, beams, Albert Speer'. For this tour Bowie again performs a sort of musical comedy, which is what glam rock always was, with the volume permanently turned up to maximum. But now, under the glare of a Speer-style cathedral of light, Ziggy, described by him as a mixture of 'Woolworth and Nijinsky', is sporting a tailored suit by Yves Saint Laurent.

The thing that really turns him on are fantasies of totalitarianism, the flipsides of power, referring in his texts, songs and interviews to acts of oppression as much as to the state of being oppressed. He is experiencing what the philosopher Günther Anders said about the world after Hiroshima: man has become all-powerful as he has the ability to bring the world to an end at any moment, and at the same time he has become powerless as he can wipe out himself at any moment, being after all in possession of the necessary weapons. Bowie is fascinated by such paradoxes, doomsday scenarios in general. He would like to make a musical of *Nineteen Eighty-Four*, but this does not materialize as Orwell's estate is opposed to it. But he continues to be obsessed with ideas of a totalitarian dystopia, a world conceived of by Bowie as a kind of Studio 54 after a nuclear attack. Instead of turning into a successful millionaire, Bowie is ruined financially and psychologically by touring. The tour, on the other hand, makes him into a superstar in America. A superstar haunted by ghosts. There's hardly a statement about him from this period, hardly a biography written about that time that doesn't mention his wild dreams, his UFO sightings – and his vertiginous consumption of cocaine and turnover of sexual partners.

Anyone coming across Bowie in this period finds it scary. It would be to flatter him to call him emaciated. His pale, bony frame weighs barely 50 kilograms. His wrists and claw-like fingers look like paper, his alien-like eyes, one bright and one dark, seem absent and his face is white, cold and expressionless. He is reputed to be living on cocaine, milk and several packs of Gitanes a day. People claim to have seen him drinking orange juice and occasionally nibbling at a piece of red pepper, but what he consumes apart from drugs can't be all that much. Bowie is living on thin air and is gradually disappearing into it.

There's a famous photo from this period. A dreadful photo that doesn't lose any of its horror however many times you look at it. It was taken back stage at the Uris Theatre in New York on 1 March 1975. Bowie has just presented the soul singer Aretha Franklin with a Grammy. Here he looks like death warmed up, a corpse in a cape and a black hat. Aretha fails to shake hands with him; perhaps it's just awkwardness. She snatches the trophy out of his hands, then says: 'This is so good, I could kiss David Bowie.' Everyone laughs and Aretha quickly adds a good-humoured apology, she meant the best – but the damage is done.

Later some of the award-winners and those presenting the awards at the ceremony posed for one more photo; Aretha Franklin is absent, as one might imagine. In this awful photo Roberta Flack, who also received an award, is standing sweetly on the extreme right-hand side. She is standing there as if she can't get too far away from the corpse, as if she has sought refuge beside John Lennon and Yoko Ono. On the extreme left-hand side is Bowie, next to him is Art Garfunkel wearing a grotesque top with a dinner jacket that has a bow tie and a button-hole in the lapel printed on it, and this fancy dress costume only adds to the ludicrous, sinister impression that David Bowie is dressed up for Halloween – as the ghost of himself. You feel like spoonfeeding him warm soup as fast as possible.

It takes some time before Bowie picks himself up out of the mire into which he is gradually slipping, brushes himself off and seeks refuge in Europe; he then draws a line under everything and moves to Berlin, not just taking on a different role but becoming a different person. This takes a little while. Perhaps a year, but a year in Bowie's then time scale is equivalent to several for other people.

British television at this point broadcasts an epoch-making documentary given the title *Cracked Actor* by its young director Alan Yentob, from a song of Bowie's. The film covers the period from the end of 1974 to the beginning of 1975 in Los Angeles and mainly shows Bowie in the back seat of his limousine driving through America at night, muttering away to himself – caught turning his nose up suspiciously every so often. In one scene in the film he is being driven through downtown LA, police sirens can be heard, and Bowie in a silver-grey jacket with hair dyed ginger and kohl-rimmed eyes, is asking: 'Do you think they're after us?'

Cut to the street, a strip mall and restaurants, night-time America under the neon glare – suddenly from nowhere a dog runs across the street, quick as a flash, a couple of seconds, the blink of an eye – now it reminds you of a scene from Michael Mann's feature film *Collateral*, that stark thriller about a killer who is driven between victims through Los Angeles at night. At one point, however, the film pauses for a moment as coyotes run across an avenue; likewise it's night-time and neon-lit, likewise the backseat is occupied by a desolate passenger, this time Tom Cruise. It may be a coincidence, a provocative one: if it proves anything at all, it's that it's as if Bowie's life was made of celluloid and reflected on celluloid and in mirrors, a *cracked actor*. The most celebrated collateral damage Los Angeles has inflicted. One image of a man. Then another. Then another. Then another.

In the BBC documentary anyway, after the dog has disappeared, Bowie in his soft, very English, nasal voice says: 'There's underlying unease here, definitely. You can feel it in every avenue. It's very

calm and it's a kind of superficial calmness that they have developed
to underplay the fact that there's a lot of high pressure here.'

You can't help thinking: there's underlying unease here,
definitely. You can feel it in everything he says. Bowie is very calm
but it's a kind of superficial calmness that he has developed to play
down the fact that he is under a lot of pressure. Bowie is not just
talking about Los Angeles, he's talking about himself. *Cracked Actor*
deals with the dangers of fame and the fact that Bowie sometimes
can't tell the difference between himself and his roles. You see him
trying on different sorts of fancy dress, you see him having a
deathmask done, arranging the ironing of his wardrobe, copying
the cut-up technique of William S. Burroughs, a writer he admires,
by composing fragmented, disjointed texts. You see him on stage
during his *Diamond Dogs* tour changing from one character to
another. 'I got lost at one point', the cracked actor says, sitting in
an anonymous hotel in Los Angeles, not in the backseat of his
limousine any more. 'I couldn't decide', Bowie admitted in *Cracked
Actor*, 'whether I was writing characters or whether the characters
were writing me or whether we were all one and the same.' Then
a bit later he adds: 'I'm very happy with Ziggy.' He laughs at this,
but when Yentob asks whether Ziggy isn't really a monster, Bowie
straightaway agrees. It's not the police but his own creations that
are after him.

Cracked Actor goes out on the BBC on 26 January 1975. It may well
be that Michael Mann saw the documentary sometime. Certainly
his British colleague Nicolas Roeg sees it at that time and realizes
straightaway who he must have for the central role in his next film,
The Man Who Fell to Earth – Bowie just has to play it. Roeg and the
scriptwriter Paul Mayersberg don't want a professional actor for
the part of the alien Thomas Jerome Newton who comes to earth
in search of water for his arid planet. They are after someone who
can portray isolation and alienation. Someone who embodies
what it's like to have quit the world or just landed on it, to look

like a humanoid but to be an alien being moving among humans but never coming into contact with them. Right from the start of his career the term 'alien' has always been applied to Bowie: he seems to have originated on another planet. 'This child has been on this earth before', the midwife is supposed to have said when she helped David into the world and saw his blue eyes, though at that time his surname was still Jones. Years later, after a fight with another schoolkid, one of his pupils is permanently dilated.

The Man Who Fell to Earth is made for David Bowie. He doesn't need to read the script to agree to it. He isn't bothered too much about the contract, he drops in on the set and gets straight down to it. Mayersberg had even included some lines from Bowie's songs right from the start, long before there was a decision on who was to play the main part.

Bowie has, however, been waiting a long time for a part in a film like this, turning it down is out of the question. He's not just a rock 'n' roll singer, he insists again and again in *Cracked Actor*. Instead he 'portrays' his songs, saying: 'I wanted my body or my muscles to play an active part in the performance.' Bowie has been a member of the actors' union Equity since October 1967. Under the guidance of his then manager Kenneth Pitt he has been trying without success to get into the theatre. Thus in 1967 he lands a part in a film – called *The Image*, no less. Finally he takes acting lessons from the gay mime artist Lindsay Kemp. He teaches him every-thing Bowie needs to know about theatrical effects and sublimation and gives him a part in his play *Pierrot in Turquoise*, playing a character called 'Cloud'. 'A kind of Bowie', Kemp feels, 'an ever-changing shape'. And he has Bowie do his song 'When I Live my Dream' on stage.

Now eight years down the road he can do what he has always dreamed of doing, work on the film of *The Man Who Fell to Earth* beginning in New Mexico in July 1975. Bowie locks himself away in a trailer and makes UFO sightings above the desert, but he gets

down to work and knuckles under, letting the director do what
he likes with him. Roeg and Mayersberg insist on their main actor
doing nothing in front of the camera but be himself. This is a lot
to ask of a kaleidoscope of a character like Bowie but he manages
it, his first film turning out at the same time to be his best.

Roeg is responsible for some unforgettable images in his
portrayal of Bowie – that is, Thomas Jerome Newton. What's
more, he develops the iconic nature of the superstar, taking
familiar motifs and inventing new ones. Take, for example,
Newton in a duffel-coat in the New Mexico desert shown
drinking a cup of water from a lake. Another one is Newton
in a centrifugal accelerator. And Newton sitting in front of six,
then twelve television monitors showing the same programme,
pictures of a chameleon for example (how often has Bowie been
referred to as a 'chameleon of pop'?), or an Elvis film, Newton
eventually shouting: 'Get out of my mind – all of you!' Newton
in the back seat of a dark limousine, muttering meaningless
orders into a car phone and wearing a fedora just like in *Cracked
Actor*; Newton as some kind of asexual naked mole rat dreaming
of male bodies and messing around with his partner in the film,
Candy Clark. 'The first movie hero to have had his crotch air-
brushed', as Pauline Kael describes him in the *New Yorker*. Candy
Clark as Mary-Lou who can carry Newton in her arms, since, she
complains, 'you're too thin'; Newton attempting to join in the
singing in a church, not knowing the words, so just moving his lips
in time to the music – a perceptive scene given Bowie's subsequent
cinema career in which his acting is often less successful. In this
case, for once, the singer is not attempting to act but the actor is
attempting to sing. The balancing act gives Bowie something to
hold on to in this role. Despite the fact that the name Newton
makes you think of the law of gravity, he drifts weightlessly
through his performance. 'Life's a Gas', his fellow glam rocker
and friend Marc Bolan might have said.

'David Bowie – phenomenon of our time', a tremolo voice
says dramatically in the trailer for *The Man Who Fell to Earth*. The
film therefore plays with ideas from Bowie's megalomaniac career
that the cinema-goers of the time would have recognized. When,
for example, Newton is offered $300 million for his inventions,
including self-developing four-dimensional film, he says flatly:
'I need more.' You would not expect anything else from Bowie at
this time. In any case it's remarkable how Roeg plays around with
the clock. One is always ticking away in the background. 'What's
the time?', Newton asks, and also: 'Is time on my side?' All the
characters are around the alien age, but not Newton. 'I wanted to
get rid of any sense of time in my film', the director explains later,
that's why he shows Newton in his limousine travelling through
New Mexico in the present but at the same time looking out on
a landscape belonging to the period of the westward expansion
of America. A year before his move to Berlin, these time shifts
foreshadow what Bowie is to attempt in that divided city: travelling
in the present while looking back to the past.

It's questionable whether Bowie is consciously aware of this.
Graeme Clifford, the editor of the film, for one thinks that Roeg felt
that 'what was going on in David's head was definitely not linear'.

You could even say that, like a nineteenth-century bohemian,
Bowie is subjecting all aspects of his life to the dictates of art. Or
it seems Bowie gets his visual ideas from all over the place. In *The
Man Who Fell to Earth* Newton is driven around by a hefty chauffeur
with a broad New York accent. This is Tony Mascia from Brooklyn,
Bowie's bodyguard, a former sparring partner of boxer Rocky
Marciano, also signed up straightaway by Roeg after seeing
Cracked Actor – and the limousine in with the deal. The following
year Mascia will be at the wheel of that Mercedes 600 taking
Bowie and Iggy across Europe with a bootful of Nazi literature.
Even when the filming was over he was 'being Newton for six
months', wearing his gear and even keeping his mannerisms.

'Now I think that David Bowie looks like Newton', he says, speaking of himself in the third person.

The distinction between the world of the film and real life is therefore blurred. Newton refuses to shake hands with people – just as Aretha Franklin refuses to shake hands with the Alien Bowie at the Grammy ceremony, and just like Warhol, who doesn't want to shake hands with Bowie on first meeting him in 1971. Newton records an album, entitled *The Visitor*, at the end of the film. We see the black-and-white picture on the cover showing a motel reminiscent of Robert Frank's photo reportage *The Americans*, famous for its portrayal of desolation. We see Rip Torn, Newton's one remaining friend, listening to the album on headphones. We don't hear the music, though, any more than we hear the soundtrack recorded by Bowie for *The Man Who Fell to Earth*. All that's left is a bass track, if we can believe what Bowie says. It resurfaces backwards in 'Subterraneans' on *Low*, the first record of what's called the 'Berlin Triptych'.

What happened? Originally Bowie's fee for the soundtrack is to be negotiated, but this doesn't materialize. Perhaps, like Newton, he needs more money; perhaps Roeg thinks Bowie's music is unsuitable; perhaps it's Bowie who backs out because his soundtrack is not going to be the only one. In the end, the music for *The Man Who Fell to Earth* is done by John Phillips.

Bowie's relationship with his manager Michael Lippman eventually breaks down over this episode: he gets rid of him just as he got rid of Tony DeFries from the MainMan agency, feeling cheated over his royalties and nearly broke. He is occupied by legal wrangles with both his former partners for the whole of 1976, bringing Bowie near to financial ruin and more or less having to buy himself out of MainMan. This, nevertheless, doesn't stop him making music at an incredible rate. Every one of his recordings is more original, more groundbreaking than the average stuff to be heard on the radio at the time.

Certainly, 1975 was a typical year in the life of David Bowie prior to the move to Berlin. Before filming *The Man Who Fell to Earth* Bowie worked on his album *Young Americans* in Philadelphia; we see Bowie's next transformation, turning this time into a soul singer made of white plastic. Then in spring 1975 he is being filmed by Roeg as an alien in the New Mexico desert, at the same time working on ideas for a new album, going into the studio as soon as the movie is finished to record *Station to Station* and finally giving all his time and effort to the soundtrack for his film that is rejected. All this takes place over barely twelve months. Bowie is productive but unhappy, above all his nerves are getting him down, he's haunted by ghosts, living in a riot of black magic and white powder and clouds of mysticism.

There's even a photo illustrating this. There's a photo of practically every dress rehearsal, makeover and stage in Bowie's life; like a television monitor, he is a medium for producing images. The carefully crafted surface is above all what Bowie is about, a creature of the stage, a performer who displays his face only in a role, not his true face but one of many. Driven like Oscar Wilde by a longing to manipulate his own image, Bowie uses his body to remake himself over and over again. Putting everything in quotation marks, he tries out experiments on his own body, applying sexual labels to it, the best example being 'Ziggy Stardust', that ambiguous creature that can be either a man or a woman, either in the past or in the future. In *Cracked Actor* Yentob asks a distraught-looking Bowie what he thinks of his fans dressing up like him; he replies that 'The idea of finding another character within themselves – that's something I feel very strongly about. That one isn't totally what one has been conditioned to think one is.' Bowie is never concerned with identity, only with roles.

'We have had the idea that contemporary art is to a certain extent about itself', Bowie tells the German edition of *Rolling Stone*

25 years later, theorizing in a way with hindsight on the excessive experimentation with his body. 'That was the opinion at the time amongst postmodernists: that's the deeper meaning of rock 'n' roll!' Bowie's illustrates this fact skin-deep on his very person. Whatever there is below the surface, whatever has been going on inside him is difficult to fathom, and anyway, from the artistic point of view it's irrelevant. 'Amazing guy, isn't he?', John Lennon apparently commented on Bowie at the time he was working with him in the studio on *Young Americans*. 'And meeting him doesn't give you much of a clue, you know . . . Because you don't know which one you're talking to.'

But going back to this photo showing Bowie as a bundle of nerves. When it is taken in 1975, he's still living the fancy dress party that is Los Angeles, at first in Beverly Hills, then in Bel Air, staying there until the spring of 1976. Bowie, thin as a rake with his hair ginger and combed back like Thomas Jerome Newton's, is stretched out in a bare, grey room, drawing the Kabbalah Tree of Life on the floor.

It must have something to do with Los Angeles, nowhere else in the world is the Kabbalah so much in fashion as in Hollywood. Madonna, who is often mentioned in the same breath as Bowie in relation to artistic makeovers, is probably now the most prominent devotee. In Los Angeles, Bowie too goes in for the Kabbalah, a school of mystical teaching of ancient Jewish origin, in its latter-day Californian version increasingly resembling a kind of pop esoteric cult. Its students wear red wristbands to ward off evil spirits. Roughly speaking, a Kabbalist believes in an all-encompassing order of numbers and letters, and the individual carrying the whole of God's creation within himself. And thus, man having access to universal forces, he himself can influence them, through meditation, by means of signs and spells, by force of will. The divine forces are manifested in stages consisting of four worlds and ten spheres and thus determine what happens in the material world – that is, in the figure of the individual who is the medium between the spheres.

The divine sphere is Kether, the worldly sphere being Malkuth, and the path leads upwards along the branches of the Tree of Life. Or as Bowie sings: 'One magical movement from Kether to Malkuth.' The line comes from *Station to Station*, Bowie's next groundbreaking album, just as the photo of the Kabbalistic skeletal figure of Bowie comes from that album.

This photo he added to the reissued CD of *Station to Station* at the end of the '90s. Another photo from the shooting of the film was printed on the cover of *Creem*, the legendary American music magazine, in December 1975 (in the same issue there is a very original report from the set of *The Man Who Fell to Earth* in which Bowie enthuses about German Expressionist films – all at a temperature of 38 degrees in the shade).

The ten-minute-long title number from *Station to Station* Bowie later refers to as 'a step-by-step interpretation of the Kabbala, although absolutely no one else realized that at the time, of course'. He doesn't get it quite right either – the divine progress is exactly the opposite way round, from Malkuth to Kether. But one mustn't be picky when a superstar is doing the talking. In his epic Bowie also plays with Shakespeare's *Tempest*, and significant certainly for his state of mind that has been heading off into outer space for some time are the quotes from the work of the occult specialist Aleister Crowley.

He was the craze of the time, just as the Kabbalah still is nowadays. Crowley was himself a student of the Kabbalah. And a heroin addict. And a pornographer. His face is there on The Beatles' *Sergeant Pepper* cover, and even 25 years later The Red Hot Chili Peppers from LA (where else?) call their album *Blood Sugar Sex Magik* after Crowley's key term. When he talks about 'magick', he means 'the Science and Art of causing Change to occur in conformity with Will'. The added 'k' comes from *kteis*, the word in ancient Greek for vagina. 'Do what thou wilt shall be the whole of the law', Crowley says. 'Love is the law, love under will.' Even if many of his devotees don't see the hedonism in this, for Bowie, the follower of Nietzsche, this comes across as all too familiar and just what he wants to hear. On *Station to Station* he invents himself anew in the shape of a cold *Übermensch*, or superman, wasting away for love.

The album contains just six tracks. The title number is brilliant, with references on the wild side, jumping about all over the place, the parts of the song fragmenting. An electronic-quadrophonic train pulling into a cabaret nightclub and stalling on an out-of-tune piano, the song then drags itself out until, after three and a half minutes that seem to last an eternity, just when you have almost given up hope that he will ever come in, Bowie starts singing: 'The return of the Thin White Duke / throwing darts in lovers' eyes' – a reference to Crowley, who in July 1918 is said to have killed a young couple with darts during a magic ritual, the whole career of the most famous magician of the twentieth century being littered with strange cases of death. Writers, from W. Somerset Maugham and Anthony Powell right up to J. K. Rowling, have immortalized Crowley in their books. He has become an icon. The most recent one to have gone in search of Crowley and his magickal commune in the ruined 'Abbey of Thelema' in Sicily is the Swiss author Christian Kracht – and Kracht immediately came under suspicion of Satanism. Powell, on the other hand, turned Crowley into a character in his cycle of novels *A Dance to the Music of Time*, the title of this cycle on its own no doubt having been a cause of considerable excitement for Bowie.

But more later on about the relationship between music and time. For the moment we are talking about Los Angeles in 1975, the year in which Kenneth Anger's famous chronicle *Hollywood Babylon* is published, a strange reference book wallowing in the sexual exploits, ritual murders, the dark side of the stars of the silver screen since the days of silent films. Of course, they know one another, Anger the movie-maker apparently even encouraging Bowie to collect his urine so he can, if need be, drink his own life juices. They meet in New York. Anger lives in an apartment on the Upper East Side, indeed resembling a shrine to Rudolph Valentino if the accounts are to be believed. It is said there is a screen hanging above the fridge, and Anger, the curator of his own Valentino retrospective, even speaks in a whisper. The director of *Lucifer Rising* also made a film about Aleister Crowley, *Inauguration of the Pleasure Dome*. Admittedly, Bowie has for a long time known about the life and work of Crowley the magician, singing about him (and Heinrich Himmler, Churchill, Garbo and Nietzsche's *Übermensch*) years before in his song 'Quicksand'. Anger is simply a spur to Bowie's renewed interest in Crowley. Meeting the director stirs Bowie up no end. Up until now it has been just a joke, with references to the 'Hermetic Order of the Golden Dawn', a magical order whose rites are based on the Kabbalah Tree of Life, used for effect in *Hunky Dory*. Now he meets someone who really shows sympathy for the Devil.

It takes some time before the images from Anger's *Hollywood Babylon* are superimposed on Bowie's own image of the city and Bowie starts calling Los Angeles 'the most repulsive wart on the backside of humanity' and 'the most vile piss-pot in the world'. Los Angeles, Bowie says later, is 'a movie that is so corrupt with a script that is so devious and insidious. It's the scariest movie ever written. You feel a total victim there, and you know someone's got the strings on you.' He says that once he has realized that it is 'the least suitable place on earth for a person to go in search of identity and stability'. By the spring of 1976 he has sussed all this out. Before that Bowie is living – shielded by his close companion Coco Schwab, who shelters him from all the world and its devices – in a Beverly Hills house, 637 North Doheny Drive, and creating images.

Imagine this really depressing scene: Bowie holding court, as described by one biographer, with Coco admitting only drug dealers and hookers on crack. There he is, sitting crosslegged and surrounded by black candles, muttering magic spells, painting pentagrams, according to another witness – and having his swimming pool exorcised by an expert in the occult. Things go on like this for some time: he is said to be living like a vampire, behind closed curtains, roadies supplying him coke by the sackload and cashing in on him, sleeping in till the afternoon and then spending day after day in the studio without a break. He makes models representing a Nietzschean *Übermensch*. Or he sits there apathetically, making swastikas on steamed-up windows. Elton John on visiting him fears that Bowie is close to death. Lennon pays a visit too, finding him sitting in the bedroom sobbing 'Why? Why?' into a handkerchief. Cameron Crowe from *Rolling Stone* interviews him, Bowie jumping up and running to the window to close the curtains, saying that he has just seen a body falling out of the sky.

The most disturbing images have, however, been provided by Angela Bowie. A long-distance call: she is in London and he somewhere in Los Angeles, he doesn't know where but, she remembers, it sounds as though her husband is talking to her from a dark place, saying that he is going to be meeting the Devil in person and that he would run away but two witches are stopping him from escaping. Angie does everything possible to discover where her husband is. In the end he manages to get away by himself – by simply taking a taxi.

In the meantime these images and anecdotes have created a whole myth about the dark side of rock, the truth of which is hard to disentangle. Even Angie, whose marriage to Bowie is beginning to fall apart at this time, has an interest in describing him as an egocentric drug fiend and herself as a caring handmaid who can coax Bowie into eating again at last. 'My chemistry must have been superhuman', Bowie says once he is in control of himself again.

I'd stay up for seven or eight days on the trot. . . . Of course, every day that you stay up longer – and there's things that you have to do to stay up that long – the impending tiredness and fatigue produces that hallucinogenic state quite naturally. Well half-naturally. By the end of the week my whole life would be transformed into this bizarre nihilistic fantasy world.

Some of his biographers have tried to put Bowie on the couch, diagnosing cocaine-induced psychosis, pathologizing him, declaring him to be schizophrenic, which is something that might be to a certain extent a family illness and is, of course, pure speculation and unfair. It is enough, however, to go by what Bowie himself says. 'You retain a superficial hold on reality so that you can get through the things that you know are absolutely necessary for your survival', he later describes this period in his life.

But when that starts to break up, which inevitably it does – around 1975 everything was starting to break up – I would work at songs for hours and hours and days and days and then realise after a few days that I had done absolutely nothing. I thought I'd been working and working, but I'd only been rewriting the first four bars or something. And I hadn't got anywhere. I couldn't believe it! I'd been working on it for a week! I hadn't got past four bars! And I'd realise that I'd been changing those four bars around, doing them backwards, splitting them up and doing the end first. An obsession with detail had taken over.

The end result of this drug-induced paranoia, bursts of activity and panic is *Station to Station*: the album is launched on 23 January 1976. On the cover Bowie is still dressed as Thomas Jerome Newton. In his brilliant essay of 1986 on Bowie, 'Der Favorit', Heinz Rudolf Kunze described its six numbers as 'Claustrofunk'.

Bowie announces the 'return of the Thin White Duke', in the opening lines of the album. But where is he returning from? Bowie presents a character that hasn't been seen before. Time is on his side.

In a scene from *The Man Who Fell to Earth* illustrated on the cover of the new album, Newton is asked whether he is Lithuanian. No, English, he replies. Bowie, the British Alien, is homesick, he wants out of the horror film that is Hollywood, longs to be back home – now all of a sudden, however, this is not located in Bromley or on Mars but in Central Europe. 'I need a change of scene and foreign places', he tells German *Playboy*. The locomotive that you can hear thundering and puffing at the start of *Station to Station* is 'the Orient Express leaving Vienna Ostbahnhof station', Kunze writes. On his train journeys across America Bowie listens to nothing but German music, Kraftwerk's *Autobahn* and the second album by Neu! from Düsseldorf. These are groups that break all the rock conventions established by the British and Americans in the same way as Bowie, now in a position to dictate these himself, at the start of his career had sought to overturn the conventions of rock. In Kraftwerk and Neu! he can make out signs of the future. Monotonous rhythms, endless repetition, strictly circular, free improvisation and, above all, electronics. Total disembodiment. Keys touched without the sound producing any feelings. Bowie is blown away by it all.

First, however, he has got to create the image he can slip into. So in 'Word on a Wing' Bowie tries it out, singing: 'In this age of grand illusion / you walked into my life out of my dreams'. A black limousine is waiting for him on the seafront at Cannes. It's not very far anymore from there to Berlin.

2 THE CABINET OF PROFESSOR BOWIE

One evening in 1968 an up-and-coming musician by the name of
David Bowie goes into a London cinema to see Stanley Kubrick's
2001: A Space Odyssey. He is carried away by the extraterrestial
images and colours, the time shifts and the story of the ascent
of man put on the screen by Kubrick to the strains of a Johann
Strauss waltz and the sharp choral atonalities of György Ligeti.
He immediately rushes home to write what would become a
worldwide hit: 'Space Oddity', the story of the astronaut Major
Tom losing contact with Ground Control and drifting off into
the universe.

We have no idea of the name of the cinema where four
years later the superstar David Bowie sees *Cabaret*. But we have
to assume that he did see it. The film is based on Christopher
Isherwood's episodic novel about the Weimar period *Goodbye to
Berlin*, published in 1935. It was to become compulsory reading
for anyone who ever indulged their fantasies, every sexual
experimenter, every would-be bohemian and timewaster, anyone
at any period feeling nostalgia for Berlin no matter where in the
world. People have largely forgotten that Isherwood's Berlin
stories were first dramatized by John Van Druten for Broadway
in 1951. David Bowie certainly saw this play – called *I Am a Camera*
– in London in the mid-'60s. As he describes it to his friend from
his schooldays, Hanif Kureishi:

The lighting was fantastic. For a long time I didn't realize that the lighting I was looking for was a kind of Brechtian lighting that created a distance between the audience and the stage. But I finally discovered that and traced it back to German Expressionist films. I started to understand a whole series of scenes I liked and the way they affected me.

He is talking here about the classic films of the '20s and '30s. 'The first film that got me', Bowie says in an interview with *Der Spiegel*, 'was *The Cabinet of Dr Caligari*. I was round about 14. Later I saw *M* and *Metropolis*, also films by Pabst and Murnau and they all came out of Berlin.' Then again another fifteen years later, during the filming of *The Man Who Fell to Earth*, these are the type of films he watches when he is in the mood. He has got them on video: 'Mostly pre-1930 German films. They're very stylised, that's the kind of film I like, but no one makes them like that now.'

Always having been keen on the imagery of German Expressionism and of the Weimar Republic, Bowie's camera eye must have zoomed in on *Cabaret* sometime in 1972 and absorbed images from the film stored away to be used later on, just as Bob Fosse's film, shot at the Munich film studios and winning Rolf Zehetbauer an Oscar, absorbs images of an earlier period and breathes new life into them. The journalist Sylvia von Harden, for example, is shown, as in a painting by Otto Dix, sitting at a table among the social elite in the Kit-Kat Club. Then there is Sally Bowles portrayed by Liza Minnelli up on stage dancing and singing 'Life is a cabaret'. If it's true that all the world's a stage, then why not come to the cabaret's tableau vivant too?

What effect does *Cabaret* have on Bowie? Michael York as Brian Roberts with his side-parting (which Bowie himself has later in Berlin). Brian Roberts on a bicycle (which Bowie himself has later in Berlin). Brian Roberts with Sally Bowles (his own version of which Bowie himself has later in Berlin). In a replay of Brian

Roberts arriving by train at Berlin Anhalt station, Bowie himself arrives at Berlin Zoo station the following year. In his case he is coming from Moscow with his friend Geoff MacCormack, only to be besieged for three-quarters of an hour by worshipping fans and by the German tabloid newspaper *Bild*. That is in May 1973, almost exactly three years before he takes the decision to make a longer stop between trains in Berlin. Could that be the noise of the Trans-Siberian Railway train that Bowie had crossed Mongolia on that you can hear at the start of 'Station to Station'?

Cabaret with its fly-by-night population, its Nazis, its drag queens and grotesque masks hits screens in 1972. It is a time of glam rock fashion when all sexual boundaries are being blurred, and right at the head of this spectacle, Bowie as Ziggy Stardust reigns supreme. The film, heaped with Oscars, shows the slow rise of the SA, the beer hall battles and street brawls. Meanwhile outside the cinema, in Bowie's home country, the lights are slowly going out all over Britain as it threatens to slide into a bottomless pit of strikes, power cuts and racism. Bowie's *Diamond Dogs* album and his tour with it are the prelude to this backdrop. But it isn't until the staging of *Station to Station* that Bowie indulges in those Expressionist elements that had made such a mark on his teenage years – represented by a harshly lit, cavernous void.

The period of incubation for this imagery is quite long. Bowie carries it around with him the whole time as part of his mental baggage. He doesn't work out any particular images until the moment comes when he is overcome by nostalgia for Mitteleuropa. He clearly feels very lonely in Los Angeles, making him long for the dream world of his youth. 'I wanted to go back to a kind of Expressionist German film look', Bowie says later. 'A feeling of a Berlinesque performer – black waistcoat, black trousers, white shirt, and the lighting of, say, Fritz Lang oder Papst. A black-and-white-movies look, but with an intensity that was sort of aggressive.' His performances in the spring of 1976 begin with the famous eye-slitting scene from Buñuel's film *Un Chien Andalou*, followed by a few bars from Kraftwerk's latest album *Radio Activity*. 'It might have been staged by Speer', the American press says about the stage show, but at the same time journalists are also a bit nonplussed at Bowie in his cathedral of light coming on like a French *chansonnier*, one Gitanes after another in the corner of his mouth, while seeming to be doing something more like an imitation of Sinatra. Who is he supposed to be? The Thin White Duke stands lording it at the mike, his hair combed back, looking cold and hard, a 'very Aryan, fascist-type; a would-be romantic with absolutely no emotion at all', as Bowie describes himself. In this period he talks a lot about Hitler.

'I think I might have been a bloody good Hitler', he says to *Rolling Stone* in February at the start of the tour. 'I'd be an excellent dictator. Very eccentric and quite mad.' Such comments are never about politics, more about image: Hitler 'used politics and theatrics and created this thing that governed and controlled the show for those 12 years. The world will never see his like. He staged a country.' Politics, performance, staging: 'It's the theatricality of Nazism rather than the ideology that attracts Bowie', is what the British cultural critic Nick Stevenson says, explaining it with reference to Klaus Theweleit's *Männerphantasien* (*Male Fantasies*). The narcissistic Führer-figure the 'Thin White Duke' suppresses any feminine desire for warmth and security in favour of iron self-discipline. It's a way of coping with all the personal problems that beset Bowie in Los Angeles, Stevenson claims, and for which he had only himself to blame thanks to his self-imposed star cult and drugs. Bowie himself says that at the time, with all the stress of the *Station to Station* tour, he wasn't quite in his right mind and all this business with Hitler and the stuff about the Führer was at the end of the day nothing but a fixation with Arthurian myth: 'The search for the Holy Grail. That was my real fascination with the Nazis. The whole thing that

in the Thirties they had come over to Glastonbury Tor.' Right
there on this hill above the Somerset Levels in southwest England
is said to be the gateway to Avalon, the realm of fable, the home
of King Arthur and the Knights of the Round Table. Being, as
he was, politically naive, Bowie claims, what he had in mind was
not the atrocities that the Nazis had committed, even if he has
difficulty understanding that now with hindsight. 'At that time
I was obsessed with the idea that the Nazis were looking for the
Holy Grail.' The charge of racism has been raised 'quite inevitably
and rightly', but 'None of that had actually occurred to me,
inasmuch as I'd been working and still do with black musicians
for the last six or seven years. And we'd all talk about it together
– about the Arthurian period, about the magical side of the whole
Nazi campaign, and about the mythology involved.'

This kind of history lesson is also witnessed by the journalist
Bruno Stein in a Chicago hotel suite in 1975. He meets Bowie for
the magazine *Creem* after a concert. Coco Schwab is there, Ava
Cherry (Bowie's black backing singer and lover at the time) as
well, and in addition three other black women, a roadie and a
guy who claims to have seen UFOS. Bowie is jumping about all
over the place, saying that he used to work for two guys who put
out a UFO magazine 'about six years ago'. And he made sightings
six, seven times a night for about a year, when he was in the
observatory. 'We had regular cruises that came over. We knew
the 6.15 was coming in and would meet up with one another.
And they would be stationary for about half an hour.' Then he
goes on a bit about media control ('they are killers, man'), cultural
manipulation and the Maya calendar, finishing up with the Third
Reich. Stein carefully notes down what Bowie says: 'Hitler, too,
was controlled. He wasn't really the man in charge.' Then he
really gets carried away: 'He was a terrible military strategist',
Bowie says, 'the world's worst, but his overall strategy was very
good, and he was a marvellous morale booster. I mean, he was a

perfect figurehead. And I'm sure that he was just part of it, that he was used . . . He was a nut and everybody knew he was a nut. They're not gonna let him run the country.' Here one of the guests points out that Bowie is the figurehead, the main man of his band just as Hitler was the main man of his entourage. Bowie gets round this by saying the responsibility is on everybody's shoulders: 'It looks like Hitler but the actual effect was produced by a number of people, all working their own strategies of where it was going to go.' Eventually everyone bursts out laughing at the absurd turn to the conversation, Bowie puts on a few tracks from his new album and then – dressed in his striking green, mohair coat and arm-in-arm with the four black women – off he goes in his limo into the American night.

There is a statement that is both original and amusing made by the Slovenian artistic pop group Laibach, who in the 1990s experimented over and again with using totalitarian iconography and have therefore been much reviled but largely misunderstood: 'We are fascists, in the sense Hitler was a painter.' During this period Bowie is a fascist in the sense that he is himself a painter – that is, maybe a bit, but then again not at all. He is being a dilettante and anything he sees in the images in front of him he relates to himself, to what he could be, a painter perhaps or perhaps a dictator, either way someone who makes the rules in their own world. All a pop star can do in a liberal democracy after all is to spread mass psychosis. All the more so if the pop star dominates the market as much as Bowie does, finally taking charge, as he is at this time, of his own management. A pop star can do this if, like Bowie, he discovers an image that stirs up desires and satisfies them, over and over again, but then not totally: the whole thing must be held on a knife-edge, otherwise all the tension is released. 'Art depends on such people', the writer Dietmar Dath says in relation to Bowie. 'What someone at home in their own skin, permanently aware of their motivations, produces is perhaps the ideal; but there is no edge, no fire, no spark to it.'

And playing with fire is one image Bowie projects, a metaphor that his art is alluding to. He can perhaps take consolation from the thought that Speer's cathedral of light wasn't after all made up of anything but rays of light that can be turned off, leaving nothing behind. Many people inhabit a world of desire filtered through the visual sense. Bryan Ferry is one such, Warhol another, and David Bowie is the same. 'Pop satisfied my visual cortex', so says the graphic designer Peter Saville, who in the mid-'70s saw his life in the album covers of Roxy Music and who himself later created iconic covers for Factory Records in Manchester. But Saville also says everyone at that time in the '70s had studied at the feet of 'Professor Bowie', on how to manipulate one's self-image and learning through this that identity is nothing but a matter of visual stimuli. It was Lindsay Kemp who taught Bowie how to perform this trick, performance venues providing a safe haven for the acting out of desires and postures without serious consequences, as both are merely for show. You only need three things, Professor Bowie teaches: *Lights, Camera, Action*.

He goes on learning himself. He tries on different costumes and comes across Christopher Isherwood's old tweed suits. On the memorable evening of 11 February 1976 the two of them meet in Los Angeles, backstage after a concert. The painter David Hockney – likewise no stranger to visual desire – introduces them to one another. Bowie sounds Isherwood out at length about Berlin; Isherwood assures him that the city was bloody boring at the time. 'Young Bowie', he says, 'people forget that I'm a very good fiction writer.'

But so is Bowie. The next day there appears in *Rolling Stone* his notorious interview with Cameron Crowe, in which he sees people falling from the sky, lights a black candle, immediately blowing it out again and above all he freely associates ideas about

Hitler: 'Girls got hot and sweaty and guys wished it was them up there. That, for me, is the Rock 'n' Roll experience.' He can't get this out of his head. He is dying to put this show on the road. A black Mercedes is awaiting him on the seafront in Cannes. Europe is awaiting him. He takes Iggy Pop by the arm and boards a ship bound for the other side of the Atlantic. Bowie doesn't much like flying, at least *that* is one thing that makes him different from Hitler. He performs as the 'Thin White Duke' in Germany, in Munich, Düsseldorf, Berlin, Hamburg, Frankfurt, Zurich, back to Frankfurt, and then Bern, from where he goes on to Scandinavia, two nights in Copenhagen. From there he goes back by sea to England, where the Press is waiting for him. On 2 May 1976 he arrives at Victoria Station by the Orient Express, climbs into his Mercedes and half-raises his left arm in a sort of greeting.

But thinking of the title of a picture by the painter Martin Kippenberger, at whose Club s036 in Kreuzberg he soon becomes a regular, we can say that Bowie for his part doesn't see anything resembling a swastika in all this. 'I'm not sinister', he insists when speaking to Jean Rook of the *Daily Express*, the only journalist allowed to interview him at this time. 'I don't stand up in cars waving to people because I think I'm Hitler.' And when all Jean Rook does is simply take the pictures and statements of the previous weeks as a whole and starts to interpret them, when, she says, he comes over as an emaciated Marlon Brando, playing at being a member of the Hitler Youth, Bowie replies: 'No, no, no . . . I'm Pierrot. I'm Everyman. What I'm doing is theatre, and only theatre.' He goes on: 'I'm using myself as a canvas and trying to paint the truth of our time on it. The white face, the baggy pants - they're Pierrot, the eternal clown putting over the great sadness of 1976.' An entertainer with make-up is performing on stage while right-wing thugs from the British National Front are brawling in the streets outside. It's just like a scene from *Cabaret*.

When, however, all the dust whipped up, the sparks and the powder have settled, we are left with two practical reasons why Bowie wants to return to Europe and live in Berlin: he needs to save money. And in '75–'76 he is mad on listening to German bands.

We can deal quite quickly with the first reason. Bowie's break with his managers costs money, though now at least only the artist himself is earning money from his music. His new lawyer advises him to go into tax exile for the tax year 1976–77. Angela Bowie looks for a house in the vicinity of Montreux, finding Clos des Mésanges, a seven-bedroom chalet in Blonay, on the northern shore of Lake Geneva. Switzerland is where the money is stashed away, the management cut back, businesses set up to oversee Bowie's artistic rights. Bowie is again free to concentrate solely on what he is really interested in: art.

American funk and soul are out, now he listens to improvisers like Can, and particularly Kraftwerk, and this is the other practical reason for being interested in Central Europe. German electronic music is the most radical thing that pop music has to offer in this period. Kraftwerk's *Autobahn*, after all, was Bowie's constant companion on the *Station to Station* tour and also in the streets of Los Angeles. He meets Ralf Hütter and Florian Schneider, the leaders of the Düsseldorf band, at one of his concerts and is supposed to have asked them whether Kraftwerk would accompany him on tour, but they politely decline. But their monotonous, disembodied, mechanical music attracts Bowie's attention, 'the costume boy' is in search of new opportunities for dressing up, leading him towards the East, across the Atlantic, homewards. He is fed up with Los Angeles, with America, with rock 'n' roll – here is a group that could not care less about America and rock 'n' roll. 'What I was passionate about in relation to Kraftwerk', Bowie says, 'was their singular determination to stand apart from stereotypical American chord sequences and their wholehearted embrace of a European sensibility.'

It is more likely that the sensibility Bowie is mad about has its roots in a totally different place than good old Europe. Neu!, for example, also from Düsseldorf, Bowie's favourite group, featuring Michael Rother on guitar and Klaus Dinger on drums, goes in very much for repetition, not like Bruckner but more like a prayer mill. Rother lived for a time in Pakistan before coming via England to Germany, and presumably it's from there, the East, that he gets his melodies going round in endless circles. This is later called a 'loop'. Rother, however, says: 'Dinger and I have never discussed concepts.' This is the difference between the two Neu! musicians and their old band Kraftwerk who, after beginning more playfully, now find expression through discipline, process and the regularities of technology. And if Rother and Dinger ever discuss concepts, it's only something like whether a chord change is needed in a song. What they mean by this you can hear for example in the number 'Negativland' on their debut album: the bass repeats the same thing for nine minutes, with Dinger's drums working out his rhythm, going around at times more slowly, at others more quickly, Rother's guitar soaring over it distortedly in the feedback. 'I've always been fascinated by stories that have no end and no beginning', Rother says. Stories in which time is abolished.

Whenever you listen to this music, you think: where have these new guys appeared from? There's lots of talk about Bowie's compulsive need and energy in his makeovers but here we are confronted with a whole series of young artists creating an unrivalled avant-garde out of nowhere. And there's been nobody to follow them up. This is a bit like the New German Cinema that around the same time achieves international success with films such as Wim Wenders's *Kings of the Road* (*Im Lauf der Zeit*) and Rainer Werner Fassbinder's *Fox and His Friends* (*Faustrecht der Freiheit*). But there's hardly anyone following in their footsteps. Who is there still playing drums like Klaus Dinger? A few techno-musicians in Cologne and Hamburg have taken up his repetitive style, and of course Kraftwerk's. But Rother says – and here he doesn't show so much regret as surprise – he even now comes across musicians in Britain and America who are seriously involved with his music. 'Nothing like this has happened to me in Germany, though.'

When his former partner and beloved arch-rival Klaus Rother dies in March 2008, Michael Rother puts an obituary on the net – in English. Jaki Liebezeit, drummer of the classically trained sound group, the free-spirited Can, says: 'We have always been accused above all here in Germany of not being able to play.' Can was another of Bowie's favourite German bands, one whose improvised specialist rock emptied a concert hall in Munich containing 1,500 people – leaving a handful of listeners behind, including David Niven, the actor and quintessential English gentleman. 'They thought', says Liebezeit describing the German public of the time, 'that we were trying to play like the British and Americans but would never be able to do it in a month of Sundays! The only people who perhaps understood that wasn't what we were doing were the British.' Among them was David Niven. And David Bowie.

But actually this is not all that odd and certainly not regrettable but makes perfect sense. It fits in with the rule Rother and the other pop musicians of the period kept to: don't follow any model, start again and again from square one, be yelling out something new, just like the group's name: Neu! 'Because of the war', Ralf Hütter explains, 'and the rupture it caused with the past, we no longer had a tradition to respect, we were free to experiment. And we weren't taken in by the myth of the pop star either. We'd seen enough of that in the 1930s.' If Bowie heard this statement in 1978 when Hütter made it, he certainly must have felt disappointed. The rejection of tradition he happily takes on board in his own break with rock conventions, translating the edginess of Kraftwerk into his own terms.

The suggestion that Kraftwerk left their mark on *Station to Station* and the three following albums, Bowie now considers 'lazy analyses', their way of working being totally different, much more rigid than his: he approaches the work expressively whereas Kraftwerk are disciplined, their rhythm lacks movement while his drummer Dennis Davis is impulsive. Besides, their *Trans-Europe Express* dates from after *Station to Station*, not the other way around, so he can't have been paying tribute to Kraftwerk. In addition it was not about railway stations. 'We were', Bowie says, 'poles apart'.

Nevertheless, the Australian writer Hugo Wilcken in his brilliant short book on *Low* has identified a number of surprising parallels:

> Both Bowie and Kraftwerk conceived of their act as a whole –
> the music, the clothes, the artwork, the concerts, the interviews,
> all integrated and self-referring. They both nodded to Pan-
> Europeanism, recording versions of their songs in French,
> German and English. Both nurtured a camp sensibility,
> working the delicate seam that lies between irony and
> earnestness. Both blended postmodern pastiche with a retro-
> modernist asthetic. Both made emotional music by seeming
> to negate emotion. Seen through the prism of psychiatry, the
> work of both comes across as rather autistic (Bowie's autism
> is schizophrenic, Kraftwerk's obsessive-compulsive).

Seen through the lens of a film camera, when in the last stages of his *Station to Station* tour Bowie throws a party in the Paris club Ange Bleu where Kraftwerk turn up, it looks rather like a scene from *Cabaret* – and in fact in the style of matinee idols of the '30s. The performance comes over now as reminiscent of Max Raabe and his Palastorchester, noted for their coolness (rather like Max Jaffa and his Palm Court Orchestra in a similar period), except that the image is shattered as soon as Kraftwerk start playing. Electronic. Minimalist. Strictly disciplined. 'Look how they are, they are fantastic', Bowie is supposed to have said to Iggy Pop. His enthusiasm is not restricted to Kraftwerk: 'I bought my first vinyl *NEU 2* in Berlin around 1975 while I was on a brief visit', Bowie recalls years later.

> I bought it because I knew that they were a spin off of Kraftwerk and had to be worth hearing. Indeed, they were to prove to be Kraftwerk's wayward, anarchistic brothers. I was completely seduced by the setting of the aggressive guitar-drone against the almost-but-not-quite robotic/ machine drumming of Dinger. Although fairly tenuous, you can hear a little of their influence on the track 'Station to Station'.

Neu! break up the year *Station to Station* is released, 1975. Dinger founds La Düsseldorf, Rother switches to Harmonia, an electronic trio with Dieter Moebius and Hans-Joachim Roedelius, who have already worked with Brian Eno under the name Cluster. At Forst in the Weser Uplands in September 1976, Harmonia even work on music with Eno, Moebius and Roedelius having met him in 1974. And it's from him that Rother and the others discover the extent of enthusiasm their music has whipped up in other countries, particularly on the part of Bowie and most of all on the part of Eno. 'We were flabbergasted', Michael Rother recalls:

> My God, they at least know about it! In Germany we were totally cut off from the outside world, everyone was working in total isolation. There were a few music magazines, sure, but otherwise we were largely invisible for the public – and the public were just as invisible for us. But recognition from the

outside world never really surprised me. The key thing was always my own enthusiasm, and if this is shared by a pop star, that's fine. We were totally convinced that our music was the right sort. We were perfectly aware that we had to be self-confident if we wanted to move beyond conventions.

'If our enthusiasm is shared by a pop star, that's fine' – you can see here the reason why Bowie eventually clears his head in Germany.

Music shunning all conventions, created electronically, in a timeless sphere – this is what Bowie tries out for himself. What could be more different from America, what would go better with the 'Man Who Fell to Earth' than asexual mechanical sounds coming out of the future? With the arranger Paul Buckmaster and some musicians from the *Station to Station* recordings he goes into the Cherokee Studios in Los Angeles some time between September 1975 and February 1976. What results has never been heard by the public, with a few exceptions. In the end, Bowie's soundtrack is rejected.

What results is, in Buckmaster's words, 'slow and spacey cues with synth, Rhodes and cello' and 'a couple of weirder, atonal cues using synths and percussion'. One ballad instrumental, he says, appears on *Low*. In an interview the journalist Mike Flood Page plays one of Bowie's compositions on cassette to Nicolas Roeg, who just arrived from Los Angeles: 'It's a simple melodic instrumental based around organ, bass and drums, with atmosphere courtesy of studio wizardry all put together and performed by Bowie himself.' Later Bowie sends his director the completed Berlin album with the note: 'This is what I wanted to do for the soundtrack.' But this is what he *wanted*, not what he managed to do. The stuff he records at this time, according to those who heard it, is interesting, but not really up to standard.

Bowie needs a partner to be able to write his new music. He has known Eno for some time. It seems they first met in 1970, according to the music historian Mark Prendergast, which was the time the American experimental composer Philip Glass came to London to perform his *Music with Changing Parts* at the Royal College of Arts. Two years later Eno appears on synthesizer with Roxy Music as a more tasteful version of the alien drag queen created by Bowie in Ziggy Stardust. Bowie's and Eno's careers run closely parallel after this. Brian Eno considers *Station to Station* 'one of the great records of all time'. David Bowie for his part is fascinated by what changes Eno makes on his solo albums, his way of slowly falling silent, and the way the sounds and electronic layers set the tone. He is particularly impressed by *Another Green World* from 1975. Bowie and Iggy Pop can apparently hum the record by heart. Also *Discreet Music*, from the same year, which does nothing but deconstruct layers for a whole half-hour, and then Pachelbel's famous Canon. Bowie listened to this non-stop on his American tour. According to Eno anyway, leaving him thinking: 'God, he must be smart!'

In any case it seems as though the two of them had been moving in each other's direction for years (just as Bowie had been moving in the direction of Berlin). Eno, who actually hates funk music, suddenly realizes through Bowie's albums, that 'if you took this a little bit further it became something very extreme and interesting'. In other words, he is moving in Bowie's direction, who is in this period in search of 'the hybridization of R&B and Electro', just as Eno wants to fuse 'this strange, rigid, stiff stuff' of Kraftwerk with the 'weird physical feeling' of the American funk band Parliament. 'When you find someone with the same problems', Eno says, 'you tend to become friendly with them'.

When Bowie appears at Wembley at the start of May 1976, Eno comes backstage. The two of them agree to work together on music as soon as possible. This is the key moment for the music on the three albums that Bowie later calls his 'Berlin Triptych': *Low* and *'Heroes'* of 1977 and *Lodger* of 1978.

Of all those associated with and aiding Bowie in the course of his career, of all the guitarists and drama teachers, all the pianists and Iggy Pops, Eno is the most intelligent, a one-off, a lucky break and, above all, an equal partner. Bowie is a dilettante, Eno a self-declared non-musician, but the two together forge a partnership in their joyous pursuit of everything new, diverse, different. 'At our regular sound-swap meets in 1976, Eno and I exchanged sounds that we loved', Bowie says. 'Eno offered, among others, his then current fave, Giorgio Moroder and Donna Summer's military R&B and I played him Neu! and the rest of the Düsseldorf sound. They sort of became part of our soundtrack for the year.'

Who played what to whom and in which order is irrelevant. They are both in 1976 reaching for the stars, or put it another way: Eno is Ground Control. And Bowie is Major Tom.

3 *LOW*, OR A SUPERSTAR'S MEDICAL RECORDS

'I have a new piece of equipment', Tony Visconti says. 'It's called a Harmonizer.' And what can it do? 'Well, it fucks with the fabric of time.'

Eno and Bowie are over the moon, a machine for playing around with the inner workings of time! It's just what they wanted. Get it out at once! The three of them get into contact with one another via a telephone hook-up: Visconti, an old crony of Bowie's, producer of *Young Americans*, is on the phone in London, the other two are in Bowie's Swiss chalet at Blonay. It's summer 1976.

Visconti has described this conversation in great detail in his autobiography. If it really happened as he describes it there, Bowie probably said something along the lines of: 'Tony, we're thinking of going into a studio for a month. We don't have any actual songs yet but we're trying to combine Brian's ambient music techniques into writing rock songs. Look, Tony, before we start recording I have to say this is strictly experimental and nothing might come of it in the end. Are you prepared to waste a month of your time?' To which Visconti is supposed to have replied: 'Wasting a month of my time with David Bowie and Brian Eno is NOT wasting a month of time.' He packs his bags and the Harmonizer, flies to Paris, gets into a limo and travels to the Château d'Hérouville, where Bowie and Eno are waiting for him with the other musicians.

Visconti knows the studios. The American, born in 1944, is a seasoned producer. Here, 40 kilometres from Paris, is where he

Helsinki, April 1976: Bowie as the 'Thin White Duke' on his European tour, Tony Mascia at the wheel of the Mercedes 600.

worked with Marc Bolan and T. Rex on their fourth record *Tanx* in 1973, likewise in the same year with Bowie on his covers album *Pin-Ups*. The spacious Château d'Hérouville dating from the mid-eighteenth century is where Chopin and his lover George Sand had their refuge. The composer was later to die here of consumption. The château has 30 bedrooms, a dining hall, practice rooms, tennis courts, a swimming pool and three studios, two of them located in a roomy extension and another in a side wing. Elton John wrote 'Candle in the Wind' here in 1973. The Bee Gees write 'Stayin' Alive' here, but not until 1977, after Bowie has already moved out. 'Stayin' Alive' could be like a motto for him in 1976.

Bowie takes up residence in the château at the end of May 1976, accompanied by his son Zowie and his Scots nurse Marion, his assistant Coco Schwab – and Iggy Pop. Here in the Château d'Hérouville, Bowie decided, his American friend is coming to work on a new record: *The Idiot*.

Bowie, Iggy and the others stay for the whole of July. They produce numbers such as 'China Girl' and 'Sister Midnight', written by Bowie when he was fiddling around with the soundtrack for *The Man Who Fell to Earth*. At the beginning of the year while still in Los Angeles, Bowie in his limo picked up Iggy Pop, stoned and psychotic, more or less on the street. He took him on tour and finally brought him to Europe. If Bowie is in a bad way at this time, then Iggy Pop is in an even worse state. Back in Los Angeles the two of them must have made a pact to get clean, to get back their health, far, far away from the hell of Los Angeles. That's where Iggy Pop, the heroin addict, had in the end admitted himself of his own free will to the Neuropsychiatric Department of the University of California, no longer able to carry on.

Some people now say Bowie exploited Iggy Pop, controlling him sexually and artistically. Some people now say Bowie saved his life. Paul Trynka, in whose biography you can follow Iggy Pop's life at Bowie's side on the road to Berlin and in Berlin in more detail, says that this friendship created the best music either of them ever produced.

Eduard Meyer, Bowie's sound engineer at the Berlin Hansa Studios, says, on the other hand: 'Iggy Pop's opinion was not decisive. The aesthetic discussions were led by Visconti, Bowie and Eno.' In the case of Bowie's records, anyway. So here are the three aestheticians in the Château d'Hérouville in September 1976 standing around Visconti's Harmonizer, said to manipulate the inner workings of time, but all the machine does is make a noise as though someone is being punched in the guts – Visconti has to admit this himself. Bowie scratches his head in disbelief. The concept is good, but the world is not ready for it.

The Harmonizer, Eduard Meyer, explains, 'was the first piece of equipment to alter pitch. A time delay shifts it either one octave up or down. In this way you can even level uneven singing voices, by passing them through the equipment which delays them and levels them automatically. We also often used the Harmonizer at Hansa Studios, but not in such an eccentric and listenable form as in Bowie's case.' Which then happens, after the three geniuses have been hanging around the equipment discussing long enough, it's the same in the case of all three albums Bowie is involved with from now on: the musicians go with the moment and see what results.

It is decided first to only transmit the mad sound of someone being punched in the guts to the drummer Dennis Davis's head-phones. His drumming away eventually activates the Harmonizer according to how loud he bashes the skins, in this way Davis starts to play the equipment as though it was an instrument. To increase the cascading effect, Visconti turns the volume control and adds a glissando. And the sound now resulting, the sound with its very first appearance on *Low*, seeming to come from nowhere and changing pop music overnight, as it were punching it in the guts, Eduard Meyer describes as sounding like: 'Tyoo! Tyoo! Tyoo!' Meyer is a classically trained *Tonmeister*, 'sound master', and so he is naturally able to explain it in the professional jargon: 'The glissando lowered the punch on the small drum down to the basement.' Visconti, for his part, says: 'I can now change pitch without changing the speed of the tape, and vice versa.' But this doesn't quite explain what happens when the Harmonizer impacts on the inner workings of time – or the tempo, the word 'time' being nice and ambiguous. Perhaps it's something like saying the Harmonizer stores a sound only to release it for use at the same moment. In a way Visconti's digital delay unit feeds back the recorded echo of a sound against itself. The sound suddenly acquires a past, but one which can be altered. He who plays with the Harmonizer is playing with Time.

The simplest thing, however, is to keep in mind 'Tyoo! Tyoo! Tyoo!' as being the best description of what it is. You can hear it in the first seven of the eleven tracks on *Low*, in 'Speed of Life' as

Iggy Pop celebrating his 30th birthday with Bowie in Berlin, 21 April 1977.
Photographed by Andrew Kent.

well as 'Be My Wife' or 'Sound and Vision'. Drums have never
sounded like this before: harsh, inhuman, like electronic toothache.
Nor has an album by Bowie sounded like this before. This 'Tyoo!'
is Bowie's message for the future but this message is by no means
a megalomaniac decree from a thin, white duke, it's a communal
effort, and a rather accidental one – thanks to Dennis Davis's
technical expertise.

Technical expertise is not really Brian Eno's style. Eno is a
confirmed anti-musician. Besides, he prefers to think things over
for a long time before he gets going. What he lacks in technical

competence Eno makes up for it in theory and strategy. There aren't many intellectuals like him in the world of pop music, paying as he does so little regard to rules and at the same time having created so many new rules. When Brian Peter George St John le Baptiste de la Salle Eno (yes, that's really what his parents christened him in 1948) starts experimenting with tape machines and sound sculptures at Ipswich Art School at the end of the Sixties, he can hardly read music. It isn't much different later on with Roxy Music – and that is in the era of showy virtuoso performances by rock bands. Eno hates these bands, he hates their cosmetic delusions of grandeur, their diva-like pretensions, their razzmatazz. He blames the 24-track tape machine, suddenly at the start of the '70s to be found everywhere in the studios, multiplying the sound. If you want that kind of thing – and many bands such as Yes or Emerson, Lake and Palmer do – okay. New technology, according to Eno, appears to tempt bands into acting 'like a bad cook who puts every single spice and herb on the shelf in the soup', that is, over-egging the pudding. This is not, however, the reason for him leaving Roxy Music after their second album *For Your Pleasure* in 1973. But Eno definitely needs more space than he has in this straitjacket to gradually develop his own music – by totally distilling it.

No sooner has he left Roxy Music than he is equally hard at it with Bowie. With each of his four solo albums produced by Eno in the three following years, Bowie moves further and further away from pop conventions. Eno's music becomes simpler, more electronic, Eno above all less and less audible. No wonder Bowie and Iggy Pop are able to hum *Another Green World* by heart – there are hardly any lyrics to sing along with on the record. Lyrics, Eno says, impose a non-musical structure onto music. 'Some sound comes so heavily laden with intention that you can't hear it for the intentions.' And all they are are love songs! Nothing but pop music! 'I want the music to be as much as possible a continuous condition of the environment', Eno says, 'in the same way as a painting is'. What he is after is aural design, music for living in, sound sculptures.

Eno starts to work using prefabricated rules. He has been an admirer of John Cage since his time at art college, just like the Cologne radicals Can are. In common with the French composer Erik Satie he has a lack of musical training and a love of systems. Back in 1890 Satie wrote background music for Paris salons, and what he set out to do is quoted with approval by John Cage in his book *Silence*: 'We must bring about a music which is like furniture – a music, that is, which will be part of the noises of the environment, will take them into consideration.' Fifteen years later Eno uses the word 'ambient' to describe this music for living in. Sounds going round in endless circles and merging with the background. *Music for Airports* of 1978 is the starting point for this, after his working with Bowie.

The idea comes to Eno one beautiful Sunday morning in the '70s while at Cologne/Bonn Airport. He likes the futuristic nature of the architecture, perhaps as a result of the architect happening to be Paul Schneider-Esleben, whose son Florian plays with Kraftwerk, a band admired by Eno. Only he finds the music at the airport awful, any old rubbish put together on cassette, and it offends his aesthetic sensibility. So he sits down and composes four instrumental pieces for piano and synthesizer, spare, bright and airy – 'Ambient Music', he describes it as on the cover of *Music for Airports*, intended to be 'as ignorable as it is interesting'. He designed his compositions to be played in real airports, and in fact they are for a month in 1981 in the Marine Terminal at La Guardia in New York, the best one being '1/1', with a piano playing away for 16 minutes and 39 seconds. '1/2' is only half the length and consists of electronically distorted voices producing an ethereal 'Aaaaah', weaving in and out of one another. '2/1' mixes these voices and a piano lasting eleven and a half minutes; finally,

'2/2' is pure synthesizer. All of them are recorded at the Planck
studio in Cologne, the Mecca at that time of German new music.
It's where Eno met up with Bowie once in early 1976 in prepar-
ation for the *Low* sessions. The new 'ambient' music therefore
originates in Germany, at a West German airport where a British
star is probably waiting for his connection to join his Harmonia
friends in the Weser Uplands. And who knows, perhaps Eno is
eventually even on his way to join Bowie in Berlin when the idea
for *Music for Airports* comes to him. This episode then might have
produced another epoch-making album.

Whether Bowie heard the term 'ambient' as early as 1976,
as Visconti claims to recall, is doubtful, but it is also irrelevant.
What Eno has already been working on, however, when he
goes into the studio at the Château d'Hérouville and later
in the shadow of the Berlin Wall, are the 'Oblique Strategies',
a series of 113 'Oblique Strategy Cards' similar to those used in
'Monopoly', created by Eno together with the painter Peter
Schmidt, containing aphorisms, instructions for tricky situations
and solving dilemmas. If you have a creative block, you simply
draw one of the cards and read what is written there, for example:

Use an unacceptable colour
Do something boring
Honour thy error as a hidden intention
Question the heroic approach
Give way to your worst impulse
Cut a vital connection

And other examples in this vein. Eno creates electronic music
around such aphorisms, as soon becomes clear in the studio
with Bowie. The card 'Repetition is a kind of change' is the
most important, sounding like the concept Rother and Dinger
had but which the two Neu! musicians never stated in so many

words. Eno's compositions are not guided by drug-inspired flashes of inspiration but by calculated intuition. In the Roxy Music period Eno had already started handing out his aphorisms in the practice area whenever there was some problem to be overcome. 'My role in Rock Music', he says, 'is not to come up with new musical ideas in any strict sense. It's to come up with new concepts about how you might generate music. It's always time to question what has become standard and established. I figure that in a way, my contribution, if it's received, it will be on a more on a theoretical basis, about suggesting greater freedom in the way people approach music.' Bowie's answer is a bit less high-flown: 'Isn't it great to be on your own? Let's just pull the blinds down *and fuck 'em all.*'

The experts are still divided about who has the greatest influence on Bowie at this time. Is it Iggy Pop, Bowie lowering his voice down to Iggy's dark timbre? Or is it Visconti, whose dab hand at the mixing desk is behind the turning point that is *Low*? Or is it really Eno and his intellectual input after all? Bowie himself isn't in any way bothered by such questions. He generously hands over copyright to drummer Dennis Davis and bass player George Murray. And he awards the whole first side of *Low* to Visconti: 'The actual sound and texture, the feel of everything', Bowie says, 'is Tony'.

But leaving aside the 'Oblique Strategy Cards', the technology and the hunt for influences and just letting the music, created at the Château d'Hérouville in the summer of 1976, speak for itself, you can make out something else on *Low*.

The first side contains seven numbers that are more sketched out than finished. Frenetic, incomplete, hurriedly carried out, not a moment's rest. The tunes shoot about like in a pinball machine. Tunes? Bowie doesn't play any tunes, he only plays with things that can produce tunes. Guitar pre-programmed. Drum broken up. Saxophone straining. The lyrics he sings are manic, shades of

Los Angeles: 'Baby / I've been / Breaking glass in your room again
. . . ', he sings. Or: 'Pale blinds drawn all day / Nothing to do /
Nothing to say.' Or: 'Don't look at the carpet, I drew something
awful on it.' Is he referring here to the Tree of Life of the Kabbalah
from the *Station to Station* cover? (Yes, he says later.) The sixth
number, 'Be My Wife', stands out, is later released as a single but
it never reaches the hit parade. 'Sometimes you get so lonely',
Bowie sings, before the guitar fades away – just like his life in
America. 'I've lived all over the world / I've left every place.'

The rest is silence. The seventh number is called 'A New
Career in a New Town' and has no lyrics. And it leaves you
speechless. A half-way house caught between the future and
the past. A farewell gesture. Does this number dream of electric
sheep? The first notes. We are back in Los Angeles, this time it's
2019: an electronic heartbeat, a fanfare of synthesizers. Then
cut to an English pub, someone playing an out-of-tune piano,
someone else on a mouth organ. It's not the soundtrack from
The Man Who Fell to Earth, it could be *The Visitor*, Thomas Jerome
Newton's record. Or else 'Blade Runner', sitting in the night at a
grand piano above the city's rain-soaked neon lights, looking at
the photos of his children, suddenly not being able to remember
whether they are real at all or other people's prefabricated
flashbacks.

But *Blade Runner* still hasn't been filmed yet, has it? This is
true, of course, but 'A New Career in a New Town' is science
fiction, predicting Ridley Scott's images. And it makes a link
to the second side of *Low*, four instrumental pieces still to
come. Ice-cold, rootless music, banging and crashing going on
somewhere underneath. The West, but seen through the eyes
of an Englishman traumatized by America. 'Good pop music
needs history', the journalist Ulf Poschardt wrote, trying to
make sense of Bowie in that period. For Bowie, however, the
history of Europe is located more in his own head than in the

atlas, the sick man of Mitteleuropa, a split personality with
withered limbs and totalitarian features, that's what I am! In the
summer of 1976 Bowie returns from the continent of a super
power that enshrined the pursuit of happiness into its founding
constitution 200 years before, he returns to an overdose of
unhappiness. And he takes unhappiness in big doses, grateful at
last to be understood once again. The elegiac number 'Warszawa',
lasting six minutes, could be a rip-off of Chopin's famous death
march – Chopin, whose château he is living in at the moment.
At the end of this piece, the first on the instrumental side of *Low*,
Bowie sings as though he is speaking in tongues. After that he
doesn't sing again, not in 'Art Decade' nor in the vibrant 'Weeping
Wall', not until the last track on the record, 'Subterraneans'. Are
those supposed to be lyrics, though? It's in a fractured language,
a death rattle.

Anyone just listening to *Low* can hardly hear Bowie any more.
All you hear is a singer slowly fading away, his lyrics getting
more broken and shorter until they disappear altogether. Then he
takes a deep breath gasping and choking, getting his voice back at
last, this time in an alien language from Mars that nobody speaks
except him. 'So-lavie di-le-jo', Bowie sings in 'Subterraneans', but
what does it mean? And 'He-li venco de-ho'? Or 'Shirley, Shirley,
Shirley own'?

It doesn't mean anything at all. Bowie, who has used his body
as an instrument up to now, nevertheless singing loud and clear,
is now using his voice as an instrument, using his worn-out body
to sing that he has nothing to say any more. *Low* tells the story of
the most iconic pop star of his day who, at the peak of his career
after two very successful and very glossy albums entitled *Young
Americans* and *Station to Station*, suddenly drops everything. Bowie
has been famous for five years. During this time he has regaled
the world with towering delusions of grandeur and outrageous
totalitarian ideas. Now he is reduced to silence.

In February 1968 at the start of his career Bowie had written
English words for the French chanson 'Comme d'habitude' that
were rejected, whereupon the song was given different words,
becoming immortalized as 'My Way', *the* Las Vegas standard
number and Frank Sinatra's signature tune. And now Bowie, the
great interpreter, has stopped singing. Instead he spends his time
with this guy who used to prance around in a feather boa and
platform shoes but is now more into things like tarot cards. Or
into collecting wood on a farm in the Weser Uplands along with
some weird Germans and playing table-tennis. Instead Bowie
hangs out with Eno in a French château, writing songs without
any traditional structure to them. Songs in which the first verse
is no longer followed by a chorus and then another verse, with
a bridge leading to a variation on the chorus; instead they are
songs in which very often nothing happens. Except that there is
at best a scratching and barely inaudible scraping sound, indicating
that those imprisoned in Eastern Europe are struggling towards
the light.

Or a piano strikes up a note.

Tuneless. Anaemic.

Over and over.

Again.

For.

Six.

Interminable.

Minutes.

Low is the most radical departure from the music of the hit
parade ever undertaken by a superstar.

To appreciate what this step meant at the time, you have only
to imagine the following: Robbie Williams, the British twenty-first
century world star, an interpreter who like Bowie once wanted to
be Sinatra, imagine Robbie Williams, this matinee idol, releasing
an album on which he doesn't sing any more but plays around with

a synthesizer. And parades his personal angst and hypochondria as part of the Cold War. Who would ever want to listen to such a thing?

No one. No, everyone would! That's why *Low* is so successful. Who wouldn't like to nose around a bit in a superstar's medical records? His new album is 'a reaction', Bowie says,

> to having gone through that dull greeny-gray limelight of American Rock 'n' Roll and it's repercussions: pulling myself out of it and getting to Europe and saying for God's sake re-evaluate why you wanted to get into this in the first place.

And then goes on: 'When I left LA I discovered how little I knew, how little I had to say. The lack of lyrics on *Low* reflects that I was literally stuck for words.' He has run out of things to say, he concludes quite simply.

The fact that Bowie presumably ripped off from Brian Eno and his solo records the idea of gradually stopping singing does nothing to reduce the riskiness of the enterprise. Eno in the first place is not a professional singer. Second, Bowie is much more famous. And he is taking a risk with *Low*, his ex-managers demand money from him, and at the same time his record label is giving him grief. He has to make economies, that's why he moves to Switzerland, and if he hadn't already paid in advance for his studio time at the château he would get the hell out of it to Berlin, but he can't afford to.

There is a trite phrase used by stars when they are tempted to throw themselves into the arms of their public: they have 'good friends' who keep them grounded and stop them going off the rails. Bowie doesn't need any good friends. His art allows him to realize himself. For a year and a half he has scaled the dizzy heights of the American star system and applied himself to the surface so thoroughly that it is now threadbare. Now what he is after is to plumb the depths, hence *Low*. This is pure kitsch, if you see it in this light.

But Bowie is clearly shattered and literally grounded. 'It was a dangerous period for me', he says later. 'I was at the end of my tether physically and emotionally and had serious doubts about my sanity.' His marriage to Angela is falling apart. When she is staying at their joint chalet in Blonay, he moves out to a hotel. In addition, the nerve-racking legal battle with his former management means he has to go more frequently to Paris for court appearances.

That's why on one occasion he is away for two days. Before going he tells Eno: 'I want you to compose a really slow piece of music, but I want a very emotive, almost religious feel to it.' Eno laid down 430 finger clicks on a clean tape, Bowie recalls. Then they put them all out as dots on a piece of paper and numbered them all, and Bowie picked sections of dots and Eno picked sections, quite arbitrarily. Then he went back into the studio and played chords, and changed the chord as he hit that number. Bowie did a similar thing with his areas. When Bowie returns from Paris, accompanied by Visconti, 'Warszawa' is finished. Eno stole the tune from Visconti's four-year-old son as he was picking out the same three notes on a piano, lost in thought. When Bowie hears the notes on the instrument, all he says is: 'Give me a mike.' And has it right away. 'He picks up the mood of a musical landscape, such as the type I might make', Eno says, 'and he can really bring it to sharp focus, both with the words he uses and the style of singing he chooses.' The words go 'So-lavie di-le-jo' and 'He-li venco de-ho'. The style of singing is engineered by Visconti, first slowing down the recording of the band and then speeding it up, so Bowie sounds like a boy in a Bulgarian children's choir. 'Warszawa', Eno says, 'is a new direction for him. And me.'

Bowie, carried away in the studio, impulsive and quick on the uptake, learns from Eno how to construct music according to a pattern. Eno on the other hand learns from Bowie that these patterns can also be successfully combined with tunes. He is thoughtful and cool-headed. Michael Rother remembers Bowie constantly calling up while he was a guest of Harmonia in the Weser Uplands in the summer of 1976 just before the recordings in France. Bowie kept asking over and over again when Eno was going to be coming. 'He'll just have to wait', Eno said. The working title for *Low* nicely sums up the relationship between the two of them: 'New Music: Night and Day.'

That's how August 1976 is spent in the studio. In the meantime the other musicians have gone, only Eno, Visconti and Bowie are left working. In the two days that Bowie and Visconti are in Paris, Eno plays around with a piano tune that Bowie actually rejected. This later turns into 'Art Decade'. But the time at the château is about to come to an end. For the reason that it's haunted! Bowie moves from his bedroom to another, as it has a corner that is creepily cold and dark. Eno is awoken at five o'clock every morning by a hand on his shoulder, but when he opens his eyes, he is alone in bed. In addition, he has a very bad cold; surely this must be Chopin's consumption! On one occasion Visconti dares to spend the night in Bowie's haunted bedroom. 'It felt like it was haunted as all fuck, but what could Frédéric and George really do to me, scare me in French?' Perhaps the words that sum up this horror story are: 'So-lavie di-le-jo.' 'He-li venco de-ho.'

The staff are on holiday, it's August in France, *fermeture annuelle*. Just to add to things, Angela Bowie shows up with her new lover, who immediately falls out with Bowie, even coming to blows, Visconti having to separate the two of them. A French studio musician supporting Iggy Pop in the sessions for *The Idiot* blabs to the Press. It's a storm in a teacup, but Bowie is furious and wants out of it, craving a bit of peace at last from the paparazzi and media, which he has been feeding with the most dramatic images for years, for he was himself obsessed with them. 'My life is not secret', he bursts out now like Thomas Jerome Newton, 'but it is private!'

Even the food at the 'honky château' is lousy – when there is any available, that is, the studio assistant once having had to be dragged from her bed late at night to see to it. On one occasion Visconti and Bowie are so hungry that they attack some stale cheese that has been left out of the fridge – and get food poisoning from it. In the end they have had enough of the whole thing. The album that none of them really wanted to make – it was intended to be carried out only as a pure studio experiment – is in any case ready for mixing.

The entry for 21 August 1976 in Eduard Meyer's diary records the first meeting with David Bowie: Hansa Studio 1, Nestorstrasse, 1000 Berlin 31, 15.00 – 22.30. It is to do the mixing for Iggy Pop's *The Idiot*. Bowie left the Château d'Hérouville in his black Mercedes. Now he moves in to a schloss in the true city of Heroes.

4 NEW CAREER, NEW TOWN

Bowie's schloss is situated in the Grunewald, the public woods in southwest Berlin. It's called the Hotel Gerhus, a lavish villa built in 1911 by the art collector Walther von Pannwitz. Some 30 years after Bowie's time there it is to accommodate the German national football team, the background to their dreams of winning the World Cup in the summer of 2006. Again it is August in Berlin, the same time of year as when Bowie arrives in his Mercedes, only now the Palais Pannwitz is no longer called the Schloss Gerhus but the Schlosshotel im Grunewald. It was also at one time called the Vier Jahreszeiten, the Four Seasons, and then it was a Ritz-Carlton, having had almost as many name changes so far in its life as Bowie himself. It is, however, already a well-known address in 1976 even though it is largely surrounded by derelict villas. Romy Haag did a striptease there for Mick Jagger when the Rolling Stones, those notorious hotel trashers, were on a tour of Germany in 1972, staying at Gerhus surrounded by kidney-shaped tables and shaded lamps, probably choosing this hotel, Romy Haag supposes, because there wasn't 'much left to smash up here'.

Tony Visconti and the musicians stay at the Gerhus when they are in Berlin, but Bowie has to save money. His assistant Coco Schwab therefore has to look for an apartment for him. There is a great shortage of accommodation in West Berlin at the time. At the Bahnhof Zoo station it's not only the drug-dependent 'children' standing in line but people waiting for copies of the

Berliner Morgenpost, the paper with the biggest to-let section. The printers are bribed to release the ads before the edition hits the streets. Nevertheless Coco Schwab fairly quickly manages to find spacious accommodation in a block of flats belonging to a certain Rosa Morath.

Divided Berlin has some famous addresses. Günther Grass lives at 13 Niedstrasse. On the other side of the Wall, the singer-songwriter Wolf Biermann lives at 131 Chausseestrasse until 16 November 1976, when he is stripped of his East German citizenship on the very same day Bowie officially finishes working on his new album, *Low*. Ever since that day 155 Hauptstrasse in Schöneberg has been a landmark in Berlin. The block of flats that Coco Schwab found for her boss is nothing special, it's rather typical of what new arrivals move into. Almost everyone who comes to Berlin has lived in such an *altbau*, as the older Art Nouveau-style apartment blocks are called, or has friends who still live in similar ones, built some

Where Bowie lived in Berlin for three short years: on the first floor at 155 Hauptstrasse, Schöneberg.

time during the period of expansion of the capital of Wilhelminian Germany, that is, before or around 1900. Down on the ground floor there are shops located on either side of the entrance; above them, behind a bare facade, there are four floors: in 1976 it isn't any different from how it is 30 years later. Inside there are high ceilings and stucco, if it hasn't been removed. Parquet or stripped-pine flooring, maybe double doors. On the outside at most a bay window, or else a small balcony. There are apartment blocks like this all over the city, in Charlottenburg, in Moabit, in Wedding, in Kreuzberg. 155 Hauptstrasse in Schöneberg is so unexceptional that it could have featured in Wolf Jobst Siedler's celebrated book *Die gemordete Stadt (The Murdered City)*.

In his book of illustrations, Siedler, at the time the literary editor of *Der Tagesspiegel*, later to become the main critic of the devastation of Berlin as a metropolis, laid the blame for the dire state of many of the areas in his home city not on the bombing *before* 1945, but on the city planners *after* 1945. He refers to Le Corbusier as 'a brother of Air Marshal Harris', the British commander responsible for the blanket bombing of German cities. Siedler writes his book the year the Wall is put up. A child of the city to his very core, he strikes such an ironic note, as despairing as it is nostalgic. *Die gemordete Stadt* is an outcry full of contradictions, knowing full well that a lot of what he says is right and good, but some of it is irredeemably elitist. On the one hand, Siedler lumps together all the elegance of the older quarters, as if Berlin had nothing but beauty to show, looking half of the time like Charlottenburg with its wrought iron. On the other hand, he points at the new suburbs with their dormitory blocks, play areas and shopping malls. 'Anti-urban' is his word for everything planned and built in Berlin since the war, above all the estates on the edges of the city.

But this is the world Bowie enters, at least in large part. 'From a distance everything looked tidy and new', writes Christiane F. about her home, Gropiusstadt in Neukölln, a good fifteen years

after Siedler. 'But if you stood between the blocks, it stank of
piss and shit. This was from all the dogs and all the kids living in
Gropiusstadt.' In the year *We Children from Bahnhof Zoo* came out
(1978), *Die gemordete Stadt* is reissued. You could swap over the
titles of these two depressing descriptions of Berlin. And just
as Bowie's songs coming out of Hansa Studios might provide a
somewhat timely and somewhat appropriate accompaniment to
the filming of Christiane F.'s story, likewise 'Sense of Doubt' or '
Art Decade' would make a good soundtrack to Siedler's camera
outings around the post-war destruction.

Of course, Siedler is familiar with the stink of Gropiusstadt,
as described by Christiane F. But he is far too sophisticated to try
and overlay this with the overly perfumed fragrances of old-time
Berlin, what Fontane once called 'mashed potatoes with chops,
both smelling of soap-suds'. Siedler doesn't want to go back to
the time of Kaiser Wilhelm, preferring instead 'an emotional city
experience', urban life as in a novel, not a loose-leaf edition. What
he would like to do is 'create old-style living with new means'.
Not so different to what Bowie wants in Berlin.

But unlike Siedler, Bowie is equally fascinated by the run-
down, anonymous quality of the social housing blocks and by the
vestiges of imperial grandeur. Wheresoever he looks, he never
finds it alienating. Instead he is attracted by it, increasingly, to
such an extent that he sees himself reflected in it. And, above all,
Bowie hears echoes of a tune he has been singing for a few years,
ever since *Diamond Dogs*, tunes expressing oppression and being
oppressed. Bowie finds both in Berlin, the triumph of some things
and the outlawing of others, often juxtaposed in the same street,
for example the walls of pre-war buildings that used to be
gleaming, and the walls of post-war buildings that were never
intended to shine.

The renovation of the facades of the older Berlin buildings
is a great concern for Siedler. Sandblasting and bulldozers have

changed the face of the city, flattening whole streets. This was, admittedly, already happening before 'Bomber' Harris, in the 1920s when they started to put into practice what Adolf Loos in *Ornament and Crime* foresaw in 1908: 'Soon the city streets will be gleaming like white walls.' Siedler already found a few such streets; page after page he shows sanded off outside walls where there had been putti, turrets, playful decoration. It is true that Siedler can still find enough examples of these, most of them in Charlottenburg, but he sets their over-the-top quality against clean lines and deadly boring efficiency. In Kurfürstenstrasse, less than 2 kilometres away from Bowie's new abode, he discovers two remarkably typical older-style *altbau* buildings next to one another, the one on the right with putti, decoration, old-fashioned showiness, the other on the left with faceless grey rendering. Something out of *Ornament and Crime*, from Siedler's perspective. The building on the left is almost identical to the one in which Bowie is living.

Bowie, however, likes the starkness of his new home. A thin white duke, nourished until recently on milk and coke, takes up residence in Adolf Loos's whitewashed streets – 'a pure white experience', as Alan Yentob, the director of *Cracked Actor*, had once said of Bowie. The Hauptstrasse is just what Bowie wants. East of the four-lane avenue and beyond the railway track is the start of what is called the 'red island', an old working-class district crammed in between railway lines, a close-knit community teeming with life, a centre of opposition during the Third Reich, birthplace of Marlene Dietrich, old stamping ground of the cabaret singer Hildegard Knef, a younger version of Dietrich. The better sort of housing in Schöneberg is situated more to the west. Over towards the Nollendorfplatz it's a bit less congested, that's where the gay quarter starts. That's where Christopher Isherwood lived from December 1930 until February 1933, 17 Nollendorfstrasse, another landmark on the map of Berlin.

Thirty years later, Bowie's apartment is occupied by a dental practice. Below it there is a tattoo parlour, to the left and right of it a Turkish takeaway, a secondhand bookshop, a mobile phone shop, a fruit-and-veg shop, an oriental bazaar, a mosque located in the back yard of a betting shop. The exact make-up of the neighbourhood is liable to change month by month, as is the norm with small traders in this part of Berlin. In 1976 Bowie is living above a depot for spare car parts. Right next door is the gay bar Anderes Ufer, 'the other river bank', now renamed Neues Ufer, 'the new river bank'. Bowie is almost in it as soon as he steps out of his building. That's where he breakfasts on coffee and Gitanes, eats bean soup, drinks whisky and, when one night the window of the Anderes Ufer is smashed in, it's where he mounts guard, later even paying for the repair. Somewhere between 500 and 1,000 marks, legend has it, but the sum is not clearly established.

It is said to have rained a lot when Bowie moved into 155 Hauptstrasse, so we'd better get in right away, straight up the staircase that he is soon to make a painting of, with its dark stairs, the carpet deadening your footsteps, holding on to the wooden banisters. Here we are, in front of the two doors to his apartment. At that time his rooms go all the way round the inner courtyard, from one door to the other. Given the shortage of accommodation, he is well off.

Eduard Meyer, Bowie's *Tonmeister* at Hansa Studios, himself living in a spacious *altbau* not far away in the Keithstrasse, is invited to 155 Hauptstrasse for a meal at Christmastime. Goose is on the menu, and a guided tour of the apartment is given for the guests. 'The kitchen was totally fitted out', Meyer recalls.

There were pans and utensils hanging on the wall, and there was a large oak table with solid chairs around it. Beyond the kitchen there was a sort of communicating room with a stereo unit and armchairs. But apart from that it was very sparsely furnished. You got the impression straightaway that Berlin was just a temporary stop-off. There was a mattress in every room. And in one of them there was an easel with a picture on it.

Antonia Maaß, the backing singer on 'Heroes' and at the time Tony Visconti's lover, can still recall the pictures in the hall. Dark, oppressive subjects, she can't make sense of them: 'I thought, he paints because it's cool', she says. Above Bowie's bed there is said to be a large-format portrait of the Japanese homosexual author and royalist Yukio Mishima, the 'Harakiri Gigolo' (Jacques Palminger's term) who committed ritual suicide in 1970.

Bowie had an army of assistants following him around in Los Angeles; now he is accompanied by only a handful of close acquaintances, chief of whom is Coco Schwab, who also lives at 155 Hauptstrasse, along with Iggy Pop. Having a small staff is part of the project. The watchword is now 'Buy your own groceries.' Bowie's prescription in his case is a sort of short, sharp shock.

Again, here is a photo to prove it. Bowie is sitting alongside his producer Tony Visconti and his *Tonmeister* at the mixing desk in Hansa Studios. He is wearing a green check lumberjack shirt. The man, who in *Cracked Actor* drove to the gas station in the California desert dressed in black, looking in that documentary as though he no longer really belongs to the human race, more a vampire-like tailor's dummy, is now wearing shirts that you can buy from the petrol station for $3. Later on they are called grunge rock shirts, after the sort of music that went all out for authenticity, for genuine *Weltschmerz*, even at the cost of one's own life. Kurt Cobain, who at the start of the '90s, a year before his suicide, covered Bowie's 'The Man Who Sold the World' with his band Nirvana, is said to have bought lumberjack shirts at a gas station. And Bowie in his green check shirt really looks now as if he is going to be stopping on his way home to fill up his Mercedes or fetch some tomatoes from the Turkish shop round the corner.

Bowie, his producer Tony Visconti and Tonmeister Eduard Meyer at the mixing desk at Hansa Studios.

And what's more, he is starting to look sort of heterosexual, perhaps the first time for years. Only his remarkable Boysie moustache – or whatever it is that Bowie is sporting underneath his nose that is slowly recovering from the cocaine – only the slightly arty look shatters the image. A hint of Montmartre, no doubt. After all, Bowie is painting once again.

In another of the photos in which he wears a lumberjack shirt, he is cheek to cheek with a couple of dolled-up transvestites in the bar at the Lützower Lampe, a club in Behaimstrasse in Charlottenburg where Bowie, Visconti and Iggy Pop are all now regulars. Right next to Bowie, 'Karmeen', whose real name is Fred Thomé (he runs the place), is smiling at the camera, with Ziggy

Stardust hardly standing out beside him. Bowie in shirtsleeves is grinning rather inanely, like a tourist arm in arm for a snap with the ladies with the deep voices, not quite sure what is happening to him, but finding it all great fun nevertheless. Bowie isn't acting anymore, he has become an observer of transsexuality. In Romy Haag's club in the Fuggerstrasse he sits in the audience watching the acts, watching Romy miming his English version of Jacques Brel's chanson 'Amsterdam' at top speed.

Perhaps Bowie is just being an ordinary person. Perhaps he is an ordinary person at last. And more relaxed, he even dares to go on a plane again, something he hasn't done for years. In a crowded place in Paris someone tries to steal his wallet; he smashes him in the face and breaks his thumb in the process. Who knows whether Ziggy or the Thin White Duke in the back of his American limo ever had any cash in their pockets? Now you can even go ahead and call Bowie up. If he ever answers the phone, that is. His friend Edgar Froese, head of the electronica group Tangerine Dream, tells the following story from 23 July 1977 on the radio station RIAS:

Presenter: And why haven't you brought David Bowie along
    this evening?
Froese: Well, I couldn't get him on the phone.
Presenter: Why not?
Froese: His phone was not working.
Presenter: Why wasn't it working?
Froese: Perhaps he hasn't paid the bill.

The presenter Olaf Leitner and Froese both laugh, Leitner reckoning that Bowie must be hard up, but Froese doesn't think so. But that is perhaps the reason, at least that's what Bowie himself says later.

This is where Berlin begins for him. A new arrival in a spacious *altbau*, with no money but for the time being starting out on a few

art projects. Thirty years later this is a typical Berlin scenario. The city is made for bohemians, would-be or real, as the cost of living is very low. In the mid-'70s West Berlin is gradually transformed into an artistic centre where, apart from those employed on cultural projects and other freeloaders on state subsidies or benefits, hardly anyone manages to make a success of anything on a larger scale. West Berlin is politically cut off and, being so inaccessible, economically insignificant. What there is, is the theatre, thriving here for the reason that people all over the world automatically look towards this remarkable schizophrenic city and its Wall. In the mid-'70s at the very time that Bowie arrives in Berlin, there begins a series of large exhibitions at the Martin Gropius-Bau, the Hamburger Bahnhof and the Neue National-galerie. Some 350,000 people from all over the world come to the city in August 1977 to visit the '15th European Art Exhibition', divided up between the Neue Nationalgalerie, the Akademie der Künste and the Orangerie of the Schloss Charlottenburg. And Bowie could easily have been the curator of it, given that the exhibition is dedicated to the 'movements of the 1920s': Dada, Futurist city planning and Surrealism. It is the first of the large-scale exhibitions that West Berlin is soon noted for. Borsig, Siemens or Osram are no longer the only household names associated with the city, but the 'Prussian' exhibitions, 'Berlin, Berlin' and 'Ich und die Stadt' (The City and Me) for the 750th jubilee in 1987 – and the permanent exhibition curated by Lothar Gall at the Reichstag, 'Fragen an die deutsche Geschichte' (Questioning German History).

And questioning German history is what Bowie does as well. For the moment, however, he doesn't go to the museums to find out the answers but to Hansa Studios in Nestorstrasse, *The Idiot* needs to be finished. That's where for three whole days Eduard

'A sort of telepathic connection': Bowie and his transsexual muse Romy Haag.

Meyer works with Iggy Pop, Visconti and Bowie – on 21 August, then the next day and then again on 28 August. Meyer's entry in his diary is evidence of Bowie's biorhythm, as he repeatedly describes the three of them beginning at 3 p.m. and working until late in the evening, the last session not starting until 8 p.m. and not finishing until half-three in the morning. 'He gets into a very peculiar state when he's working', Eno says. 'He doesn't eat. We would be staggering home at six in the morning, and he'd break a raw egg into his mouth and that was his food for the day, virtually. We'd sit around the kitchen table at dawn feeling a bit tired and a bit fed up, me with a bowl of crummy German cereal and him with albumen from the egg running down his shirt.'

And even if he is only allowed on one occasion to sit at this kitchen table at 155 Hauptstrasse, Eduard Meyer now counts as the most sought-after witness to Bowie's time in Berlin. He is interviewed whenever television programme makers around the world mark Bowie's birthday; he is the source of information whenever journalists need juicy details about Hansa Studios for their articles or want to know what it was like when Bowie looked out of the window at the Wall from the studio control room. Meyer started in February 1976 with 'Edition Intro', a sub-label of the Meisel publishing house that owned Hansa Studios. The first thing he does is to make a record with Ilse Werner, the Dutch-German actress and singer. Later she raves about the fact that she never heard such beautiful whistling as on Meyer's recordings. Immediately the next job is David Bowie. But as the Studios are quite big, Meyer is employed on other things at the same time, one minute deconstructing rock with Bowie and Eno, the next working on conventional hit-parade stuff. 'I knew', Meyer now says – in the meantime he has retired and is living in a small town in the east of Westphalia – 'I knew that Bowie was a famous person. But I didn't roll out the red carpet for him. I wasn't a Bowie fan, I listened to classical music.' How come, then, that they collaborated so closely? 'I was down-to-earth and certainly the one who had the best English', Meyer replies. 'I was the translator, the go-between for the whole studio outfit. This gradually led to a musical collaboration.' As it happens, Bowie and Meyer both know Edgar Froese, who can't get Bowie on the phone as the line is dead. Meyer had already worked with Froese's band, Tangerine Dream. It was the Berlin electronic musicians, Meyer thinks, who probably recommended Bowie try Hansa Studios. 'Bowie and the others were horrified at the conditions at the Château d'Hérouville.' But the Meistersaal studio and the other rooms in Köthener Strasse near the Wall are booked when they arrive in Berlin in August. So *The Idiot* is first finished on Nestorstrasse, a street off Kurfürstendamm, not far from Lehniner Platz where the 'Schaubühne' are to take up residence a few years later. Then it is on to the main studio near the Wall for *Low*.

It was planned to divide *Low* into two, Meyer says. Bowie simply decided to put the fast, vocal numbers on the first side of the album and the slow, instrumental ones on the second. According to their mood, people could choose between what was accessible and what was less accessible. This you could also call choosing between brightly coloured and dark, manic and depressive, between one side of the Wall and the other.

'The backing tracks were done first, the rest was added', Meyer explains. Two numbers are created more or less anew in Berlin; for 'Art Decade' Tony Visconti has done an arrangement for chamber orchestra that Meyer now works on with his cello. 'Weeping Wall' is the only number created from scratch in Berlin. Bowie writes it on his own. 'He works with a lot of concentration', Meyer says. 'He works it out in his head. He didn't have any score, just definite ideas as to how he wanted a number.' But he also takes on board material that he comes across, leaving it up to the moment, as in the case of the Harmonizer. 'In the case of "Weeping Wall"', Meyer recalls, Bowie 'worked with a vibraphone lying around in the studio'. The instrument zings through the piece repetitively, accompanied by a nagging guitar, sounding vaguely like Simon and Garfunkel's version of the folk song 'Scarborough Fair', at least that's what Hugo Wilcken claims in his book on *Low*. In the case of 'Subterraneans' Bowie copies what he has recently learnt from Eno: 'Give me a mike, I'll count now', he apparently said to Meyer. 'Then he counted up to 200, a good five to ten minutes, later simply saying to Visconti during the counting "Drop me in at 89!"' And then he came in with 'Share bride failing star / careline / careline / careline / careline driving me / Shirley, Shirley, Shirley, own. Share bride failing star.'

Bowie, not long after his arrival in Schöneberg, comes up with titles for the free-associating electro stuff that he created in France and finished in Berlin. 'Subterraneans' is about 'the people who got caught in East Berlin after the separation – hence the faint jazz saxophones representing the memory of what it was', he tells the *Record Mirror* in 1977. 'Warszawa' is about 'Warsaw and the very bleak atmosphere I got from the city'. 'Art Decade' is 'West Berlin – a city cut off from its world, art and culture, dying with no hope of retribution.' '"Weeping Wall" is about 'the Berlin Wall – the misery of it.'

These are intelligent descriptions. They still shape how Bowie's Berlin music is seen. It's difficult to avoid going along with them. In the case of 'Always Crashing in the Same Car' on the first side of *Low*, Bowie told a nice story about him sailing along Kurfürsten-damm in his Mercedes and suddenly seeing a drug dealer who had conned him and stopping to run into his car repeatedly; 'for five or ten minutes' it went on, he says 25 years later. In the evening he is supposed to have driven round and round in circles at top speed in the underground car park of the Hotel Gerhus, with Iggy Pop in the seat next to him, until he had used up all the petrol in the tank.

Wonderful stories. And they have been told so often that they now belong to myth. Anyone who met Bowie at that time now speaks about it as though they are reading from a book in which he is being quoted, mostly quoted to confirm stories that have been related elsewhere. Bowie learned to create texts according to the cut-up technique from Burroughs; in *Cracked Actor* he showed how to do this. He writes down sentences, cuts them into strips and then sorts them again into verses. There is probably therefore no such thing as a straight solution either to his music or to his lyrics or titles, just a mystery consisting of that which the eye of the beholder constructs like strips of text – but no truth. Truth has been done away with, Ziggy Stardust saw to that (along with the Sixties). It's the same as with Isherwood: people often forget what a good storyteller Bowie is.

When he is not in the studio, he drives around the city. Soon he buys a bike, a Raleigh, the classic British make, a three-speed. Having had his breakfast of coffee and Gitanes at the Anderes Ufer, Bowie cycles down Hauptstrasse in the direction of Hansa Studios on Potsdamer Platz.

At that time this was a relatively simple matter. Hardly anyone remembers traffic jams in the '70s in West Berlin. So Bowie cycles off, past the Kleistpark underground station; after this the four lanes are no longer called the Hauptstrasse but the Potsdamer Strasse. On the left there is the Allied Air Security Control Centre, formerly the Prussian Supreme Court, where the conspirators of the 20 July plot were tried before the Volksgerichtshof, the Nazi Supreme Court. Then Bowie passes by what is termed the 'Sozialpalast', the Social Palace, a twelve-storey machine for living in built on the ruins of the Sports Palace where in 1943 Goebbels called for 'Total War' and where there are now 514 rented apartments made of concrete, to the joy of Wolf Jobst Siedler. A few hundred metres further on is the overhead railway; the next turning on the left is Kurfürstenstrasse, where an equally joyful Siedler discovered the renovated facade of an *altbau*. A few blocks further and over on the Reichpietsch bank of the Landwehr Canal

Hansa Studios at 38 Köthener Strasse, right by the Wall. When Bowie was here, the historic artists' building was half in ruins.

Bowie has on the left the Neue Nationalgalerie by Mies van der
Rohe, and the next building site on the right is Hans Scharoun's
Staatsbibliothek, the National Library. It is finished in 1978. During
the recording of *'Heroes'* Bowie can more or less watch it going up.
Here he turns right along the Landwehr Canal and into Köthener
Strasse. Number 38 is Hansa Studios. It is situated right opposite
the Wall. Right by Potsdamer Platz, the largest non-place in the
divided city.

And when he doesn't go by bike, autumn 1976 having
been particularly rainy, perhaps then he goes by bus. 'The public
transport system', Eduard Meyer says, 'is something he appreciated
and enjoyed'.

But what a route it was to take every day! It's like a cross-
section of his world of images. Bowie starts out two or three
blocks away from where Marlene Dietrich was born. Then past
a control centre of the Cold War, where the strategy of brinkmanship – escalating a situation to the brink in order to gain an
advantage, as for example in the Berlin Crisis of 1958 – is precisely
what he exhibited in all his artistic activities. Right after that he
goes past one of the memorials to the propaganda of Goebbels,
the Nazi he once intended to write a musical about, and proceeds
straight into the centre of the art produced in the period that had
interested him ever since he was a child. From there he goes
through a concrete desert towards his own present at Hansa
Studios. 'You could see', Meyer says, 'how fascinated he was, to be
living in the place where the whole story of the Nazis had taken
place. His feelings were immediately reflected in the surroundings.'

His surroundings are equally reflected in him as well. The
Hansa Studios building, constructed between 1910 and 1913, is
where the avant-garde publishing house of Malik, which belonged
to John Heartfield and his brother Wieland, was located in the
1920s; likewise the gallery of Georg Grosz, whose portrait of Silvia
von Harden was transferred to the screen in *Cabaret*, though Bowie

can't stand him. Tucholsky appeared here in 1921, as is recorded in the archive of the house and its Meistersaal, the name of the large hall on the first floor where Bowie is now working on the freely associating words of *Low*. Here under the decorative ceiling of the Meistersaal is where the SS held their festivities and celebrations, so dear to Bowie's biographers. Visconti once even claimed that 'Hitler had a lot of his propaganda music recorded in this room.' And that in the basement of the building studio technicians had found replacement bulbs for the old Neumann microphones with swastikas engraved on them. In his memoirs, mind you, the really rather genial Tony Visconti talks of Berliners shouting like Nazis in Hollywood films ('Hey Fritz! Komm hier!'). This sounds less like the Third Reich, more like *'Allo 'Allo*.

The building on Köthener Strasse was destroyed by bombing in the war, after which it was slowly rebuilt, the Meistersaal being for a short time a failing theatre, then it became a ballroom, the Susi Ballhaus. The enormous building also held a cinema, frequented particularly by East Berliners until the advent of the Wall brought a sudden end to this pleasure in August 1961. Immediately after the war, music had been recorded in the Grüner Salon, the Green Room, the place where in the photo Visconti and Eduard Meyer are sitting at the mixing desk with Bowie in green check. At that time it was the Bertelsmann organization that did professional production there, with names such as Rudolf Schock, Zarah Leander, Ivan Rebroff.

The Meisel publishing house purchases the building in spring 1976. There is a Gypsy-style encampment in the back courtyard, with dogs roaming around. When Eduard Meyer first sees the studio, all the floors below what is called the Bertelsmann Studio and the caretaker's apartment are home to birds, derelict and empty. There are no dividing walls. In the Meistersaal, soon dubbed by Bowie 'The Big Hall by the Wall', the ceiling is covered with wire mesh to stop plaster falling off: health and safety regulations. 'The windows on the right were boarded up with nails', Meyer recalls; 'in front was a drum box. There was a thick curtain hanging all the way from the stage to the entrance. We tried to record dampening the sound but to no avail, the hall was still there in the background.' In other words, on *Low* and particularly on *'Heroes'* you can hear an echo resonating from the place with Bowie in the middle. This peculiar, semi-restored building, with its faded glory, nothing quite as it should be, a temporary space for creating art, is like a microcosm of Berlin.

You can still see this today if you stand in front of the building on Köthener Strasse, with Potsdamer Platz behind you. This is the worst that the New Germany has to offer, jerrybuilt new blocks, theatres putting on nothing but musicals, a soulless shopping mall, the Debis Tower, undergrowth on the wasteland along the underground railway embankment. Right opposite Hansa Studios, Deutsche Bahn (German Railways) have one of their offices. A deadly boring building on a deadly boring spot. Every new layer adding to the former layer seems to give way immediately to the next before it is even finished. Bowie was in search of this dynamism, in which all the remains of the day live on in the same place and at the same time – and he found it. 'I've written songs in all the Western capitals', he says in July 1977,

> and I've always got to the stage where there isn't any friction between a city and me. That became nostalgic, vaguely decadent, and I left for another city. At the moment I'm incapable of composing in Los Angeles, New York or in London or Paris. There's something missing. Berlin has the strange ability to make you write only the important things – anything else you don't mention, you remain silent, and write nothing . . . and in the end you produce *Low*.

5 THE PARTY ON THE BRINK

In the year after the Wall was built, the philosopher Ernst Bloch writes a new afterword to his book *Erbschaft dieser Zeit* (*Heritage of Our Times*). It is a difficult work, a collection of essays by a dedicated Marxist that was first published in 1935 while he was in exile in Switzerland, written, as it were, under dark storm-clouds. That, at least, is the impression Bloch's images give. The book returns again and again to one central idea: 'Not all people exist in the same Now.'

Bloch calls this 'non-contemporaneity'. And however vague and esoteric that may sound at first, it is a political slogan: 'Depending on where someone stands physically, and above all in terms of class, he has his times.' The present is fragmented into different versions of the past. The farmer is rooted in the ancient soil and the eternal cycle of the seasons. The middle class in straitened circumstances want to go back to pre-war times when they were better off. The land-owning Junkers in the eastern territories are still in place, even if their economic situation belongs to the past. You can tell this was written in May 1932, nine months before the conservative forces of the Harzburg Front embraced Hitler in order to depose Reich Chancellor Brüning, the beginning of the end of the Weimar Republic.

If, however, everyone is living in the past, as Bloch claims, then who is living in the present? The proletarian, is Bloch's reply, 'desperate plight is born purely of the present'. The proletarian knows he is a possession in a world of possessions, looks forward to a future free of the conditions of production, a future that is still being withheld from him by capitalism, and thus he is living in the present time with and within the present-day crisis.

Wind forward 30 years and in the aftermath of a terrible catastrophe we find a Wall in Berlin, missiles in Cuba . . . So it is in the middle of one of the worst years of the Cold War, therefore, that Bloch adds some disenchanted statements to his book. 'But the times from which the present book emerged', Bloch writes in 1962, having in the meantime become a professor in Tübingen,

> are still vividly in the air. Their vividness is even growing, especially among young people, who never experienced them and who miss them in an almost sentimental way instead, in keeping with the term 'Golden Twenties', and the other, incidentally older exaggeration that until the night of 1933, Berlin was the intellectual capital of the world.

Which is where we come back to David Bowie. This petit bourgeois with his fear of poverty, moving to Berlin to save money, fantasizing about the Nazis and trading on his body, turning it into a consumer product – this Bowie would have been despised by Bloch in 1935. Nothing, after all, but a mass-produced artist, and then he is mad on – of all people – the German Expressionists! It is after all their reputation and intellectual heritage that the then exiled Bloch argues about with his friend Georg Lukács.

Bowie's fantasy life, however, would have been familiar to Bloch, it's exactly what he described a few years later in *The Spirit of Utopia* as a characteristic of modern man. Man, as Bloch sees him, is a being with inadequacies that strive for fulfilment and is therefore never finished, he is only ever becoming. Just like Berlin, you might say. Just like Bowie. Then there is this quotation about

The Cold War: Bowie in front of the Neue Wache by Karl Schinkel, now known as the 'Memorial to the Victims of Fascism and Militarism' in the Unter den Linden, East Berlin.

not all people existing in the same Now! Bowie goes on to sing one or two numbers about this every month that he is in West Berlin. Their titles are 'Sons of the Silent Age' or 'Subterraneans' or 'Art Decade'. What again did the midwife say who brought Bowie into the world? 'This child has been on this earth before.'

If you remove the Marxist element from Bloch's way of putting it, at the risk of causing him to turn in his grave, then 'non-contemporaneity' describes fairly accurately Bowie's state of mind in Berlin. The thing that attracts him is German pop music, which he finds the most innovative stuff going. What he discovers is the Expressionist Berlin of the dreams of his youth, the setting for which is still in existence. Anything recorded at Hansa Studios is pointing out the future. The hands of Bowie's watch are turning in all directions. It's just like *The Man Who Fell to Earth*, Bowie driving around in his limo among the ruins and the new buildings, looking at where people lived in the past.

The Berlin Bloch had known and described in *Heritage of Our Times*, the Berlin of the '20s, seemed extraordinarily 'contemporaneous, a constantly new city, built hollow, on which not even the lime becomes or is really set'. This vacuum arising from the collapse of bourgeois culture, Bloch claims, is now a place for experiments. By the time Bowie comes to Berlin to experiment 40 years later, the vacuum has only increased. Berliners live there contemporaneously with crisis, but their city is a remarkable jumble of different periods that Bowie wanders through in his waking dreams.

He is surrounded by a strangely shattered present in which the post-war period in particular lives on. Barely 500 metres from his apartment in Schöneberg, in Heinrich Kleist Park, there is the Prussian Supreme Court where after the War the Allied Control Council and later the Allied Security Headquarters are located. Bowie cycles past it every time he goes to Hansa Studios. His son Zowie attends the boarding school for the personnel of the British occupying authorities. He himself often goes through Checkpoint Charlie to East Berlin, and every day he works right by the Wall. The historian Timothy Garton Ash, who studied in West Berlin from July 1978, once summed up his journeys to Eastern Block countries as: 'I flew British Airways . . . Departure: 1983. Arrival: 1945.' That's how David Bowie must have felt.

'Berlin had to live up to the Isherwood myth', says Ash, who also writes about the 1970s in his memoir *The File*, describing from the perspective of a sceptical analyst all the romantic illusions Bowie has about the city. The parallels are remarkable, Ash coming to the city to do his doctoral thesis on 'Berlin under Hitler', living for a time in a similarly spacious *altbau*, in his case in Uhlandstrasse. He even frequents the same places, yet another exile at the Paris Bar and Chez Romy Haag. Whether the two young Englishmen, one a historian, the other too, in a manner of speaking, both of them suckers for nostalgia about the Weimar period, ever bumped into one another in Berlin we don't know. Either way, Ash's memoir is haunted by the sort of characters in Bowie's songs (and the later *Gigolo* film): ageing Prussian noblewomen, fresh-faced correspondents from Oxford in gloomy, rented rooms. Ash even acquires his own Sally Bowles in the shape of Irene Dische, a young Jewish American of German extraction who has come to the divided city to write, something she has so far been very successful at. 'Of course she had us down as Auden and Isherwood', Ash writes, describing himself, Irene and his gaunt correspondent friend James, 'or was it Spender?'

These expats take up residence in the shadows of a bygone world as the shadows are becoming longer and longer. Imagine the confusion of coming to a city that reflects to such an extent its own myth! And what a gas it must have been! I'll be your Isherwood to my Spender. Berlin all but reflects its own myth. In the parallel world, what's called real life, we find Ash and his friends coming across surviving '68ers, theorizing about structural violence while smoking roll-ups and reading Bloch.

The contemporaneity of the non-contemporaneous – that is to say, that which is not the present is nonetheless present – goes further than that, though. Bowie's rantings about a strong Führer coming to the rescue of a run-down Britain don't just come out of thin air. On the contrary, the same storm clouds are brewing over the British Isles as were hanging over Bloch's dark warnings in *Heritage of Our Times*. In the mid-'70s many Britons are reckoning their country is on the road to becoming a Weimar Republic. Mass strikes, inflation, public debt . . . Now we know that Britain was never on the brink. But people thought and talked differently at the time.

When British miners go on strike in the winter of 1973–4, the government of Prime Minister Edward Heath institutes a campaign: 'SOS – Switch Off Something', to save power. This meant, as Nick Hornby once wrote, 'that you often spent the evening eating sandwiches and reading by candlelight'. A highly developed European country in the last quarter of the twentieth century where floodlights and neon advertising are banned, where homes and offices go without heating and television closes down at half-past ten in the evening. It must have been quite a scare, and a national shame to boot.

In July 1974, at the very time Bowie is on the road in America, wasting a spectacular amount of power on his *Diamond Dogs* tour, General Sir Walter Walker writes in a letter to the *Daily Telegraph*, 'The country yearns for a leader.' Sir Walter is not just any old knight, he was once in overall command of NATO forces in northern Europe. And he heads the 'Unison Committee for Action', a group of bankers, lawyers, businessmen, soldiers and politicians; parts of the British establishment are therefore playing with fire. Sir Walter is publicly considering a coup. 'The patience of some of us is beginning to wear thin', he warns in his letter.

Margaret Thatcher, soon to become prime minister, places herself
at the head of such protest groups – not, however, to overthrow
the political order but to bring an end to the welfare state.
She is loyal to the Constitution, but nevertheless the historian
E. H. Carr compares her to Adolf Hitler.

It's open season for comparisons with the Nazis. And in the
light of this apocalyptic mood gradually twisting political rhetoric
into turmoil, Bowie's outbursts about fascism suddenly don't
seem all that way out, even some of the experts around are
talking in similar terms. He is not concerned about the present
state of Britain, the historian Carr adds, but what happened in
Germany in the Thirties. The economics columnist Peter Jay
blames the increasing budget deficit and inflation in Britain on
the current oil crisis – just as Germany suffered from having
to pay reparations to the Allies after the First World War.
The prevailing mood is therefore that of Weimar.

We know now that the crisis was being talked up; around
this time even a Nobel prizewinner like the economist Friedrich
August Hayek, advising the new prime minister that she can
after all carry out her new economic programme in a dictatorial
fashion, like General Pinochet in Chile. 'I am certain we shall
achieve our reforms in our own way and in our own time',
Thatcher corrects him. Ernst Bloch would not, however, have
been surprised. Or rather he would have been anxious to see
the proletarian, who is the one having to suffer this crisis, revolt
against the ruling powers and put the clocks right that have either
been ahead of or behind the times.

It is a matter for speculation to what extent David Bowie is
concerned with the state of the country in the mid-'70s. The two
years before his move to Berlin he had after all spent mainly in
America, not in Britain. Certainly, he enjoys the questionable
nature of what is in the air as it appeals to his imagination: until
now he has just been at a party, now he is right there, really on

the brink. And perhaps he is just talking it up, because he finds it amusing – as in the notorious interview with Cameron Crowe eventually published in the German edition of *Playboy* in January 1978, in which he wants to put an end to oppressive liberalism with 'the progress of a right-wing, totally dictatorial tyranny'.

In that interview Bowie's thoughts are all over the place. If one moment he claims that all rock stars are fascists, this is true only for as long as it takes to say it, or it's true only on stage. 'I'd adore to be Prime Minister', he tells Crowe. And now in May 1976, shortly after his controversial wave at Victoria Station, he appears at a series of London concerts as David 'Winston' Bowie. Winston as in John Lennon's middle name, or as in Churchill's first name, or as in the name of the central character in *Nineteen Eighty-Four*, Orwell's parable on totalitarianism that Bowie wanted to turn into a musical. Bowie's middle name is not, however, Winston, but Ambiguity.

A party on the brink – this is still true for the Berlin of the mid-'70s. But we are not talking about *bierhaus* brawls, mass strikes and stormtroopers but the way a city cut-off by the Cold War stays alive. It is true that there has been a measure of détente and things have considerably quietened down since Willy Brandt's Ostpolitik treaties with the East. Freedom of movement has been improved for West Berliners by the Four Power Agreement of 1971, traffic between East and West becoming normalized and more relaxed. It is the first time for almost twenty years that Berliners on both sides of the Wall can phone one another. Cutting off road links, ultimatums, harassment and blockades are a thing of the past. But the status of the city is still in the balance and this does not change until the reunification of Germany in 1990. Do the Western sectors of Berlin belong to Federal Republic of Germany? Or is the whole of Berlin an autonomous unit, as the powerful men in Moscow have always insisted? These are vital questions in the Cold War, the two blocks rubbing up against one another in Berlin like nowhere else. The Four Power Agreement in fact gives a No answer to both of these questions, but the arguments continue. Meanwhile at the Wall shots are still being fired and the 'security checks' on transit routes are being stepped up by the Vopo, the East German 'People's Police', Berlin is definitely not at peace.

In November 1977, Bowie's *'Heroes'* has just been released. The Soviet ambassador in East Berlin complains about Dietrich Stobbe, the Mayor of West Berlin, having declared in an interview that West Berlin was a part of the Federal Republic, that is, West Germany – something that was of course denied straightaway by Stobbe. What seems to be a legal quibble, however, has an immediate effect on the traffic between East and West: there is an increase in harassment, and if the supply routes don't run freely and without disruption, before long it can seriously hit a city at its very heart. As it is, 1977 proves to be a bad year for the economy of West Berlin. Bowie may well have sensed this and have turned this ambiguous, dynamic situation into artistic energy. *'Heroes'* is released in the 'German Autumn' of 1977. This 'Deutscher Herbst' is a set of events associated with the kidnap and murder of industrialist Hanns Martin Schleyer, president of the Confederation of German Employers' Associations and the *Federation of German Industries*, by the Red Army Faction (RAF) better known as the Baader–Meinhof Gang, and the hijacking of the Lufthansa plane *Landshut* by the Popular Front for the Liberation of Palestine. Following the release of *'Heroes'*, the *New Musical Express* asks him whether he had sought out the feeling of living on the brink: 'That's exactly right', Bowie replies.

I find that I have to put myself in those situations to produce any reasonably good writing. I've still got that same thing about when I get to a country or a situation and I have to put myself on a dangerous level, whether emotionally or mentally or

'Back to a kind of Expressionist German film look': Bowie in Berlin, April 1976.

physically, and it resolves in things like that: living in Berlin leading what is quite a spartan life for a person of my means, and in forcing myself to live according to the restrictions of that city.

Berlin is a divided city, struggling for its identity and a city into which meaning can be read at will, not just by artists but also and especially by politicians. A few years before Bowie moves to Schöneberg, Lou Reed already recognized the metaphorical opportunity of this, recording *Berlin*, a concept album about his marriage breaking up, about a separated drug-dependent couple, about body politics.

Lou Reed has still never once been to Berlin when he creates the album, adding to the mythology of this city that acts as a vacuum to be filled with interpretations. But Angela Bowie can remember the time she first heard her husband talking about German Expressionism and the Nazis, when he comes to London in the summer of 1972 with Lou Reed and Iggy Pop. On that occasion the three guys are sitting around taking drugs and talking sixteen to the dozen about Berlin during the Weimar period – here you can't help thinking of just what Bloch has to say about young people who have an almost sentimental nostalgia for what they never experienced.

Or, rather, what they haven't *yet* experienced. The punk rocker group The Buzzcocks later called this phenomenon 'Nostalgia for an age yet to come'. At the time all this is going on, pop music was only just entering the era of retro references that blurred the distinction between contemporaneity and non-contemporaneity. Pop songs make these terms irrelevant. They are obliterated, even if only for three minutes, because everything is merely the act of performance, contemporaneously uniting sound and vision, and also because its power of expression doesn't end with the notes but lives on as an image in theory ad

infinitum, thanks to visual references such as fancy dress or
masks. 'What is radical about Bowie', writes the cultural critic
Nick Stevenson, 'is his grasp that his music was likely to be read
through his image and not through the other way round.' For
example, when in 1971 on the cover of *Hunky Dory*, Bowie pushes
back his long hair like a star of the silent movie era in 1920s
Hollywood, he is not just undermining the macho posturing of
his rock rivals in the hit parade, he is also signalling that pop
music is at the same time a work of art and a consumer product,
and that the iconography of a star is always fabricated. In the '70s
pop music starts to become self-reflexive.

Posing like a star of the silent movie era, on *Hunky Dory*
Bowie is contemporaneously singing about life on Mars. 'Not
all people exist in the same Now', Bloch claims. But in pop songs
they are, or it is truer to say: a pop song can unite everyone's Now
from the moment in the past up to now in a three-minute present.
It's the same in the case of Roxy Music. In 1972 Bryan Ferry's band
appear in clothes combining Pin-up, Rockabilly and Radio Music
Hall, a Gesamtkunstwerk made up of material nicked from every
period and given a retread: sentimental ballads, rock, and sounds
of the synthesizer, heard for the first time, sounds coming out of
the future. This gives rise to that elegantly ambiguous figure Brian
Eno, wrapped in a feather boa. At the same time this sexual tease
is only a further move in the game of retro references. This,
according to the graphic designer Peter Saville, was the very
moment the Postmodern was born.

On one occasion Eno is observed in drag sitting on a London
Underground train, totally absorbed in William Shirer's *The Rise
and Fall of the Third Reich* (another of these foreigners in Berlin,
just at the time the Nazis were coming to power). The motivation
behind everything that is new during this period in pop music is
the very sexual ambiguity that is also surrounding Eno. Sexual
ambiguity is the high art of referentiality. If sexual roles are

arbitrary, then so are all the other signifiers, and they can be arranged in multiple combinations in a free-for-all. Bowie turns his back on his fictional characters when he comes to Berlin – Ziggy Stardust along with Aladdin Sane and the Thin White Duke. The true success of these roles, however, lies in the sexual ambiguity that Bowie is playing around with and nothing that happens in Schöneberg changes this either.

In January 1972 *Melody Maker* quotes him saying 'I'm gay and always have been, even when I was David Jones.' It's totally irrelevant whether that was ever true or whether Bowie is trying this statement on, just like the knitted overalls and the drag outfits he wears on stage. 'Camp' is the term, the lie that tells the truth. And even now this tension is the source of speculation as to Bowie's sexual preferences, it's also the source of his artistic creativity. It's his 'modus operandi', as the American cultural critic Shelton Waldrep writes, ever since Bowie acted in Lindsay Kemp's theatre group in the late '60s. Kemp combines elements of avant-garde performance traditions with dance, design and Japanese kabuki theatre, but particularly with homosexual self-realization. This can be acted out on the stage in a secure environment without necessarily having any consequences in real life.

In the real life of the divided city Bowie succumbs to the attraction of Romy Haag. The Dutch transsexual had come to Schöneberg via Paris and New York and opened her club there in a former hookers' joint on the corner of Welserstrasse and Fuggerstrasse. In her autobiography, Romy claims she met Bowie at a concert in the Deutschlandhalle on 10 April 1976. It must have been the same concert that Christiane F. attended with her junkie friends, later recreated in the film *We Children from Bahnhof Zoo*, the best-ever film scene about a concert, according to Quentin Tarantino, the body politics activist and *the* artist of retro references.

Funnily enough, the scene in that film is so reminiscent of
the episode in Romy Haag's book that one is almost like an
illustration for the other. 'We were rather stoned', Romy relates,
'and we were standing in the front row with the groupies' – in
other words, exactly where Christiane F. is in the film after having
had a few puffs on a joint with her friends. Above her head Bowie
is singing 'Station to Station' on stage, and then, Romy continues,
Bowie comes 'to the edge of the stage. He bent over, saw me, was
stunned, and I smiled.' Christiane F. too in the film stares at her
hero as if hypnotized; 'a sort of telepathic connection is set up',
Romy says, 'and I felt as though I would come to know everything
about this person.' In the case of Christiane F., however, it
is exactly the other way around. 'In the last few weeks when
I had already totally lost it, this "It is too late" spoke directly to
me. I thought the song described my situation exactly.' All this
may have been coincidence – or just the next chapter of a myth
that is writing itself over and over again.

Either way, the same evening both Romy Haag and David
Bowie end up at her penthouse (and Christiane F. at the drug
disco Sound). An intimate party with friends, Romy writes,
becomes a 'very tender night', after which Bowie has no desire
to travel the next day to Hamburg for a concert. When he does
eventually arrive there, he immediately calls her up from the
hotel: 'I really need you', he told her. 'You inspire me.' And even
if the nature of the relationship remains rather vague, it being
above all their private business, the second statement in any case
is true. Bowie found in Romy Haag an almost perfect recreation
of Sally Bowles, and in Chez Romy his Kit-Kat Club. His
imagination must also have been stimulated by the fact that
Romy, like Sally, is living at the time in the vicinity of the
'Ku'damm', the Kurfürstendamm, in the Rankestrasse.

Just how strong the tide of nostalgia at Chez Romy must
have been is described by, of all people, Angela Bowie, who talks

quite openly in her two books of bitter memoirs about Romy and her husband having a sexual relationship. 'Walking into that place' (Romy's club), Angela Bowie recalls,

> was like going back decades, to the Berlin of Christopher Isherwood, the glory days of avant cabaret before Adolf, the Soviets and the Americans turned underground Berlin into little more than an anything-goes meat rack. Romy was *very* wild and *very* sophisticated.

And within a short space of time her club has become a high spot in the nightlife of Berlin. As regards its celebrity and its extravagance, Chez Romy at this period could be matched only, if at all, by the one called the 'Dschungel', the Jungle.

That's where in January 1978 a high-school student is waiting at the club on Winterfeldtplatz, having arranged to meet someone there in the evening. It's half-past midnight, and the Dschungel is still empty, but even so the young man is not allowed in. He comes from West Germany and, with his black roll-neck sweater and angelic long hair, he looks like a student of theology. Today Cord Riechelmann is an author living in Berlin and has made a name for himself as a philosopher and biologist. At that time he had hitchhiked to the Tunix Congress at the Technical University three months after the 'German Autumn' and the many deaths arising from it. At the Congress, splinter groups from the German left-wing counter culture are meeting to hold discussions about unorthodox and especially non-violent alternative politics. In addition, the founding of a left-wing daily paper gets off the ground, going on sale a bit later as *taz*. The archive of the time may be full of happenings, theatrical events and raves, but Riechelmann chiefly recalls the transvestites and the gay activities that he comes across while attending the Congress – things he had never witnessed before. Among the participants he particularly remembers a bald man in a white roll-neck sweater who eyes him up. He passes by him on three occasions; the bald man at one point winks at him, and finally his beautiful companion speaks to Riechelmann. She is called Heidi Paris, a publisher with the Merve publishing house, and the bald man is Michel Foucault. The three of them arrange to meet that evening for a beer in the bar at the Dschungel.

The French theorist had published the first volume of his epic work *The History of Sexuality*, which appeared in German in 1977 and in which Foucault describes the concept of 'sexuality' as a discursive invention, designed to sanction deviations from the norm and standardize and control human beings, just as Foucault sees discourses as instruments of social regulation in general. The philosopher is still largely unknown in Germany, and Cord Riechelmann had never read anything by him. If anything, people at that time see in Foucault nothing but an unpleasant nuisance. That's exactly how his remarkable head (and the white roll-neck sweater) appears in the German edition of *Playboy* in January 1978, some 32 pages further on from Cameron Crowe's famous crypto-fascist interview with David Bowie.

The caption to the picture of Foucault belongs to a series of photos about 'Sex in 1977', and it says everything:

> *Sex enslaves. Sex is the whip of the powerful.* These are the defiant statements of the Paris left-wing philosopher Michel Foucault (50) that are shocking people. What's more, he has threatened to expand his theory of torture into six volumes. Bonjour Tristesse.

In the end there were not six volumes, only three, but that is of no matter. More interesting is the fact that in this January of 1978 Foucault and Bowie get to know one another better than simply on paper. When Heidi Paris and Foucault eventually put the

waiting Riechelmann out of his misery and go with him to the
Dschungel, David Bowie and Romy Haag are there.

They may well not have spoken to one another, Riechelmann
can't quite remember. These two characters meeting is, however,
the next chapter in the myth that is writing itself again and again,
as strange as Romy seeing Bowie through the eyes of Christiane
F. Both Foucault and Bowie after all share an interest in sexual
ambiguity. One of them does research into hermaphrodites, the
other turned himself into one in the shape of Ziggy Stardust.
Now in Berlin he seeks out the transsexual Romy, just as in
London a few years before he used to do the clubs in the
company of the notorious transsexual Wayne or Jayne County.
Both Foucault and Bowie see sexual emancipation as a means
through which one is free to define oneself or reinvent oneself.
What Foucault sought to work out in the later volumes of *The
History of Sexuality* is not a 'theory of torture', as *Playboy* has it,
but as he put it, 'a way of being or better still: a technique of
living. The key thing was to know how to define one's own life
for oneself, so it can take the most beautiful form possible.' In
those pages ahead of Foucault in that edition of *Playboy* Bowie
says: 'The point is to grow into the person you grow into.' And
where does what Bowie is already living, and Foucault is thinking
his way to, come from? From Friedrich Nietzsche: Become who
you mean to be.

In Bloch's vacuum for experimentation, created by techno-
logical progress and the collapse of bourgeois culture and of
course by war, is where both of them find what Cord Riechelmann
calls their 'homeground'. Foucault came to this recognition in the
Dschungel; indeed, his visit to Berlin at the turn of 1977–8 signalled
a turning point in his thinking as a philosopher. Everything he
sees on the day of the Tunix Congress and at night in the clubs,
the hermaphrodites, the sexual ambiguity, the paradigm shift,
comes to him as a revelation that whatever happens here sexually,

there is no going back. What he sees going on here are 'people working in the cause of beautifying their own life'.

David Bowie is only one of them. In his apartment on Hauptstrasse in Schöneberg, somewhere in the maze of rooms, there is an easel. Bowie grows a beard like an artist. When he is not in the studio by the Wall, writing music with Brian Eno that breaks free of all pop conventions just as they have both liberated their sexuality from all conventions, that's where he is to be found, painting, wielding his brush in the style of his heroes Ernst Ludwig Kirchner, Otto Mueller and Erich Heckel. Not all people exist in the same Now.

6 DID YOU SEE DAVID BOWIE?

The artists of Die Brücke, Brian Eno once said, painted with 'very rough, tough strokes – and they all have a mood of melancholy about them or nostalgia, as if they were painting something that was just disappearing.' And their 'boldness of attack, the unplanned evolutionary quality of the images, and the over-all mood – remind me of the way David works.'

Anyone attempting to retrace the steps of Eno's friend David Bowie in Berlin, anyone in search of eyewitnesses and references and relics, of Bowie's brushstrokes from the period between autumn 1976 and spring 1979 at 155 Hauptstrasse, is not doing anything different to what the object of their search was himself doing at the time. Bowie is in search of himself in the city. He sees himself in relation to it. 'Berlin is a skeleton that aches in the cold', Christopher Isherwood wrote. 'It is my own skeleton aching.' Bowie must have identified too clearly with the strange fate of the city. The fate of having become great, politically and architecturally, too quickly and therefore condemned to suffer growing pains for ever. The architectural critic Heinrich Wefing once spoke of a 'precipitate delivery', of bursting hurriedly into life. Having to be more and then more and more, having always had to struggle to define one's own role and still having to – Bowie recognizes all this in himself. And like Bowie, Berlin has indulged itself too much and ruined itself through megalomania. And again like Bowie the city has to pay for it with a permanent hangover. Karl Scheffler's gloomy, hackneyed dictum that Berlin is condemned eternally to become, never to be, takes on a new meaning in Bowie's case. Because Bowie is the embodiment of this statement. It's as though it were tailor-made for him. The 'ever-changing shape' is what Lindsay Kemp, that man of the theatre, called his pupil David back in the 1960s. Bowie finds a new master in the shape of Berlin.

And doesn't he just go crazy for Berlin, head over heels! The city, he enthuses, 'was the artistic gateway of Europe in the Twenties and virtually anything important that happened in the arts happened here.' He spends hours walking by the lake at Wannsee, or cycling, visiting places associated with the Nazis and has his photograph taken there – at least that's what he does in the first few weeks. He crosses over to East Berlin again and again going through Checkpoint Charlie in order to see the Berliner Ensemble, at Brecht's old theatre. Just round the corner from there he goes for a meal with Iggy and Visconti to the Ganymed restaurant on Schiffbauerdamm, which Visconti calls a 'time machine' where the other guests look like something out of the drab 1950s – this, though, is just what's termed 'really existing socialism'. Back on the other side of the Wall, in the blazing Western neon of Kurfürstendamm, Bowie is regularly found collapsed in the gutter from the effects of litres of König Pilsener, no doubt his contribution to the binge culture Berlin is noted for in the late '70s and early '80s.

Nevertheless, the city is accepting and tolerant of him just as it has tolerated every freak and engaging nutter chancing their luck here, as it always has, asking no questions, showing no great sympathy, shrugging its shoulders. After Los Angeles, Bowie says, for a time so great was his paranoia that he couldn't walk along a street without fear of people. Now nobody looks at him for longer than need be.

'Boffie' is still many Berliners' nickname for him; they called Isherwood 'Issyvoo' in the Thirties. Celebrities don't count for much in this city. 'Let whoever wants to come for all I care', is still one of the maxims of Berliners. It takes even the local newspapers some time in autumn 1976 to realize who it is that is suddenly living in Schöneberg, is a regular at the restaurant Exil on the Paul-Lincke riverbank in Kreuzberg and at the Paris Bar on Kantstrasse, and goes backstage at Romy Haag's. Who has a disconnected telephone and wants to be left alone. 'I thought I'd take the stage set, throw it away, and go and live in the real thing.'

You can see by his face that Berlin is good for him, the longer he is there, the better. You only have to compare the video of 'Be my Wife', the single from *Low* that turns out to be a flop, with the one of 'Heroes', with only four months between, from June to September 1977. But the mask that he is still wearing in the case of 'Be my Wife', the white-faced Pierrot who has applied the great tragedy of the period onto his thin skin, playing the guitar in a White Cube, a quarter of a year later in the case of 'Heroes' has turned into a serious man. Here he is, standing alone in front of a blank background, but now it is dark, shrouded, softening his contours. Bowie is still thin, but his cheeks have filled out, and he seems to have regained a hold on life. He comes across as being more dedicated. As though he has turned over a new leaf and put his image at the service of art, as if the character that he has been up to now has now become of secondary importance, in the light of the task ahead. In the video and on the cover of *'Heroes'* Bowie is wearing black leather. It's proletarian leather, Brechtian leather, severe but costly. Bowie would have been a poor disciple of Brecht if he hadn't also been just as calculating in his use of the writer's downmarket appearance as a studied affectation. The worker in the service of art – all this is is the next role.

Clearly the self-imposed reality check now works. The Thin White Duke returns – and his masquerade collapses. 'Suddenly',

Bowie says later, 'I was in a situation where I was meeting young people of my age whose fathers had actually been ss men. That was a good way to be woken up out of that particular dilemma. I came crashing down to earth when I got back to Europe.' Once on the Wall that he is soon to be singing about, Bowie is supposed to have discovered a piece of graffiti of his name – the last two letters forming a swastika. He wasn't at all pleased at this.

And as for a drug detox, Eduard Meyer recalls that only beer was allowed at Hansa Studios, 'Berliner Kindl' in small bottles. As regards what happens after work, he can't testify to that. Angela Bowie admittedly describes Bowie as having been drunk or well on the way to it every time she visited him in Berlin. Once, he has had such a skinful that he collapses in Angela's arms. She calls the emergency doctor from the British Military Hospital, a spokes-man for whom announces the next day that a woman had called in the early morning to say that her British husband was having a heart attack. 'Though we don't usually admit non-military personnel', the spokesman explains, 'as an act of mercy we sent out an ambulance to get him. He'd just overdone things, and was suffering from too much drink. We ran various tests and proved he hadn't had a coronary.'

It doesn't happen very often any more that Angela is with Bowie, looking after him. Soon it doesn't happen at all any more. The couple decide to divorce. Bowie commutes between Blonay and Berlin as it suits him. Angela claims he never even asked her whether she wanted to live with him in Berlin. For Christmas 1977 there is an unsatisfactory coming and going between Berlin, Blonay and New York, between the father, the mother and Zowie, amid missed phone calls and public rows, kidnapping and cold, and the result of it is that Angela tries to commit suicide. In the previous year she had made one attempt to stop things going from bad to worse, according to her two autobiographies, in particular trying to defend herself against the growing influence of Coco

The first part of the 'Berlin Triptych': *Low* is released on 14 January 1977.

Schwab. She says she begged Bowie to fire his ever-present
assistant but he wouldn't hear of it. And then when everything
was completely falling apart, the two women had a row, no telling
what it was about, you could say more like skirmishes over the
right to wield influence over Bowie, ending with Coco storming
out of the apartment in Schöneberg. Bowie later phoned her
upset and then followed on after her. He leaves his wife occupying
the apartment. At which Angela goes into Coco's room, pours
vodka over Coco's clothes and tries to set fire to them, unsuccess-
fully, so she throws the whole lot out of the window from the
floor below onto the street pavement. Bowie's liberal marriage,

the object of sexual speculation for years, comes up against the hard facts. She writes that she 'called a cab and caught a flight to London. And for David and me, that was the end.' At 6 a.m. on a November morning in Berlin.

Bowie goes on to write a few of these scenes into *'Heroes'*, in 'Blackout', for example. But this takes a while. Though not very long, as Bowie continues to be very productive, no change on that front even when the amount of cocaine decreases. But first *Low* has to be released, not such an easy task. On 16 November the album is finished, it's supposed to be in the shops for Christmas, a stocking-filler. But before everything is over, Bowie has his thirtieth birthday, 8 January 1977. The whole gang celebrates in Romy's club. It's not until a week later that *Low* is released, coinciding with one of the most miserable months in the Berlin calendar. In January the city shows its grimmest face, piled high with dirty snow. Something that nicely reflects the gloom of *Low*, but Bowie is upset over the delay.

What happened? Bowie's label, RCA, got cold feet. The London head office is frightened of losing money with *Low*. And Bowie's former manager Tony DeFries, who still has a share in what Bowie earns, thinks so too. Following on the success of *Young Americans*, which along with 'Fame' is to reach Number One in America, and the equally successful *Station to Station* album, this new Berlin electro stuff might put off newly won fans unnecessarily. So RCA and DeFries delay releasing the album until after the Christmas sales, in order to smuggle it onto the shelves on the quiet. So that ideally nobody notices. Bowie's new piece of work is launched in the off-season of the commercial year.

The bosses were no doubt gobsmacked when they first heard the tapes of *Low*. They must have fallen silent like Bowie on the second side of his new album. And when they managed to get their voices back, one of the managers is supposed to have said:

'I'll buy him a house in Philadelphia' so he 'can go back and make *Young Americans II*'.

The pop critics find themselves similarly challenged. That's the case for the NME, because they come out with two reviews in a row, one critical and one in praise, something that had never happened before in the history of the official journal of British pop music. The critical one is a damning indictment, Charles Shaar Murray calling *Low* pretentious, negative, totally vacuous – and that's from a real fan. The one in praise, on the other hand, hails it – 'The ONLY contemporary Rock Album' – and so in the end all these dumbfounded critics agree that *Low* is about the real present. Music for the times. The future. And if one of the bad reviews claims to see the Huns behind the music from Berlin, it's only the sort of knee-jerk reaction you get habitually from British football reporters.

Bowie is really very annoyed at the critics, but Eno is the one who says frankly: 'They are so bloody thick, sometimes I could drive nails through their heads.' On the question of whether Bowie felt unsure and possibly regretted having been silent on the second side of *Low*, Eduard Meyer shakes his head. 'That's just how he chose to do it', he says. 'Bowie needed to do it like that, and wasn't talked into it by anyone.' Even if RCA intends to smuggle in the album with the fans and fool the critics, *Low* achieves brilliant sales and reaches Number Two in the British hit parade and eleventh in the American charts. The challenging 'Sound and Vision' even turns into a real hit.

Once *Low* was finished and on sale, the crew at Hansa Studios have worked on it so long that 'Visconti could do it in his sleep', according to Meyer. 'They didn't really need me any more.' And so he only pops in again from time to time when the others begin nine months later to record *'Heroes'*. He becomes an observer. But during the period they spend together he witnesses two of the events that have come to be part of the mythology about Bowie in Berlin, images that determine what we think we know about the Bowie of that time.

One of the anecdotes concerns three young women who come to Hansa Studios one day 'after work' (Meyer) and who Bowie had met somewhere in the course of his 'evening activities' (Meyer again). There the three ladies are, standing in the doorway of the control room. 'They were rather attractive girls', says Meyer. David has a look, says 'Hello' to them first and then to Iggy Pop: 'Okay, you can choose one.'

This story has been told over and over again, summing up nicely as it does Bowie's freewheeling lifestyle. 'There is evidence', Meyer says, 'I was there.' Meyer is a serious man, as a Westphalian from the East of that region, a man of few words, he laughs indulgently when speaking about Bowie's fans who 'want to get to know their hero from the inside'. And if someone like him, this seasoned *Tonmeister*, who knew intimately all the stars who had recorded at the studios, speaks of Bowie as 'David', then it's worth taking notice. But this 'evidence' that he comes out with here is a bit odd, anyone would think that Bowie was some kind of supernatural phenomenon. If you were to mount a survey of Berliners asking 'Did you see David Bowie?', even normally rational people go a bit soft in the head and claim that they once saw him on the train passing through Bahnhof Zoo station. Bowie, a strange phenomenon. But then again, has he ever been anything else?

The other anecdote is so good that Eduard Meyer once even has to act it out, taking on the roles, 30 years later in that very same place, Hansa Studios, for a Danish film crew on the track of Bowie in Berlin. It is really good as it puts in context Bowie's brinkmanship, this teetering on the brink that he enjoys in Berlin. 'Above the mixing desk there were lamps hanging from the ceiling', Meyer relates.

And on the right there was a window from where you could see right up to the Wall as the new building opposite dates from later on – 150 metres, as the crow flies. Just down the Köthener Strasse, past the Art Academy and over some waste ground where there was a circus. On top of the building on the Stresemannstrasse there was a gun-post. The border guards could look right over in our direction. The windows were wide open, as it was summertime, and they could even follow exactly what was being recorded, the same piece over and over again.

The Vopo, the People's Police, were therefore treated to a crash course on Eno's artistic efforts, for free and outside (or inside) the gun-post. 'On one occasion I said to Bowie and Visconti, they are looking right at us through their powerful Russian binoculars. So I took one of the lamps and pointed it in the direction of the Wall: Look, there they are, the Vopos! I said. I found the two of them cowering under the mixing desk shouting "Edu, don't do that!"'

Bowie doesn't have anything to fear, though. Even if he is, from the East Berlin point of view, a typical example of a hostile, reactionary and decadent element, the Stasi aren't interested in him. They don't take seriously what he has to say about Hitler, and that's probably for the best. In the archive of Stasi files anyway there isn't anything about Bowie in Berlin during the years between 1976 and 1979. And that's despite the fact that at the time he is repeatedly driving over in his Mercedes to East Berlin and further into the GDR. Despite the fact that he poses provoca-tively in his Gestapo overcoat in front of the guard at the Neue Wache, the 'Memorial to the Victims of Fascism and Militarism, the building by Schinkel on the Unter den Linden. Despite the fact that he writes a song about the shame of the Wall and the noise from his studio echoes out over the 'Anti-Fascist Protection Wall'.

The view that Meyer illuminated on that occasion, out of the window and down the street towards the Wall, is precisely the view that Bowie's fans look for in vain from Hansa Studios 30 years later. But there's nothing there. Just the blank wall of a building.

'David enjoyed this atmosphere of a city on the frontline', Meyer says. 'He felt at home here. Berlin was very provincial at the time. It had none of the flair it has now. Due to the Wall and nobody being able to get out, it felt like an island, and David liked that.' He even starts to settle down. He paints, sticks prints of his pictures in photo albums, listens to Vivaldi and watches the evening news on television.

Meyer loves above all to tell the story about when Bowie, Visconti and Iggy Pop visit him in his *altbau* apartment on Keithstrasse, an occasion recorded in Meyer's guestbook, on 16 October 1976 (even if Tony Visconti at first writes '1975' and then crosses it out three times; it goes to show how you can lose all track of time when you are in the Berlin of Bloch). Iggy Pop wishes to be remembered by the universal toilet wall saying 'I was here'. Visconti composes a four-line verse about Edu and his wife and relating to East and West. Bowie, on the other hand, wants to put something jokey, writing 'Could I interest you in a new hoover?' This, it is true, turns into a real joke only when Bowie, in August 1978 during his visit to Club so36 in Kreuzberg, is taken for a toothpaste rep by some young punks like Thomas Schwebel. Perhaps, though, Bowie is once again years ahead of the punks.

The punk movement, which reached its peak in the summer of 1976 with the Sex Pistols, Bowie in a way misses out on. Punk, particularly the German version, sounds to him like 'post-1969 Iggy', as he says. What he finds interesting in Berlin is the art world. A bit later on the promotion tour for *'Heroes'* in autumn 1977 he tells the young British actress Suzy Bickford he next intends to go back to painting. His music, as Meyer sees it,

'Bowie has created more or less like a work of art, in the same way as you place a canvas on an easel and then fill it in.'

Near Hansa Studios, just left down Köthener Strasse on the corner of Reichpietsch river-bank, there is now a sign indicating the distance to places: 'Bauhaus-Archiv Berlin 1,750 metres', is one, 'Memorial to Stauffenberg [one of the officers who plotted to assassinate Hitler] 1,200 metres', 'Kulturforum [complex of museums, concert halls and libraries] 800 metres'. This is Bowie's idea of Berlin: radical twentieth-century modernity along with its destruction, the war, the dead, what is left after it has been blasted, then painstakingly reconstructed. Its reconstruction takes shape before Bowie's very eyes at the Kulturforum with Scharoun's Staatsbibliothek, the National Library. Back at the Château d'Hérouville in France Bowie had forced illustrated books about Erich Heckel onto the studio musicians in the breaks. Now he sees the genuine Heckel pictures for himself; it's a bit further away, so he takes the Mercedes to the Brücke-Museum.

And that's not all. Bowie, who started collecting art early on, buys Die Brücke works in Berlin, for example from the gallery owner, Artur Vogdt, he acquires a preliminary study for Emil Nolde's *The Three Kings* and the 1912 coloured woodcut *White Horses* by Erich Heckel. His Heckel, Bowie somewhat bluntly tells Leopold Reidemeister, director of the Brücke-Museum, is much better than the one in the collection in the Grunewald.

He says he bought his pictures in small galleries, at unbelievable prices, it was wonderful. One of these small galleries is called Warschau (Warsaw), and is located on Kurfürstendamm. It belongs to the hotelier Artur Vogdt. He is the son of the architect Arthur Vogdt who built a brilliant block of apartments on Kottbusser Damm together with Bruno Taut, the famous modernizer of the city, but only the facade of the building had survived by 1977. Artur Vogdt, born 1910, is a key figure in divided Berlin. One of his German teachers was the publisher Peter

Suhrkamp. Later he runs the dining hall of the Prussian State
Theatre on the Gendarmenmarkt in the period when Gustaf
Gründgens is artistic director there. After the war he works at
the Pension Continental at 53 Kurfürstendamm, which eventually
he buys. It is said that he once throws Herbert von Karajan out as
he will not tolerate any collaborators in his establishment. Young
German film directors such as Alexander Kluge, on the other
hand, are welcomed by him. The Hotel Continental, occupying
the whole ground floor, now called the Askanischer Hof, is thus
attached to the Galerie Warschau where Vogdt deals in recent
Polish art, but also some choice discoveries, works by Cocteau for
example, or the Heckel woodcut and the Nolde study bought by
Bowie. He finds in Artur Vogdt the embodiment of the whole of
twentieth-century Berlin, from the First World War through the
Second and the Cold War and right up to the present with its grey
Wall. Vogdt for his part says that 'David Bowie knows more about
Expressionist art than 90 per cent of the young people here.'

Bowie copies the rough, bold strokes of the Die Brücke
artists with his own hands, transforming Heckel's motifs into new
formats. Bowie's interest is most awakened by a series of portraits
called *Roquairol* that Heckel did in Ostend in 1917 while stationed
there with his ambulance unit. *Roquairol* shows Ernst Ludwig
Kirchner writhing in a state of nervous collapse, with his left
arm catatonically contorted. This is how Heckel portrays his
friend in a woodcut and in oils. Bowie first attempts to copy this
motif 60 years later for the cover of *The Idiot*. Initially he just
intends to have Heckel's painting photographed, then he decides
on a black-and-white picture of Iggy Pop, in a grey jacket with
arms identically contorted. The picture is taken by Andrew
Kent, who also photographed Bowie at the blown-up bunker
of the Führer and in his Gestapo overcoat in front of the Neue
Wache. Following that, Bowie puts his friend Iggy and himself in
approximately this *Roquairol* pose on canvas. 'I'm painting pictures

nobody wants to buy', he admits, 'but I love it'. Finally he portrays Kirchner's catatonic state itself on the cover of *'Heroes'*, the only album of the Berlin Triptych really to come out of Hansa Studios. *Roquairol* reflects the overall gloom of 1976. And of 1977 too. Today the David Bowie archive claims that the main influence for the cover of *'Heroes'* was another coloured woodcut by Erich Heckel, the *Männerbildnis (Portrait of a Man)* from 1919, of which there is also a copy in the Brücke-Museum collection. The parallels with the cover are clearly there – a man in black, hands clasped in front of his chin, a serious haggard face, a trace of melancholy around the closed mouth.

More interesting for Bowie's project of drawing on Expressionist sources in Berlin is nevertheless, however, the comparison to *Roquairol* – which has also left its mark on the cover of *'Heroes'*, e.g. in the weirdly stiff position of the arms and hands that Bowie adopts here. Basically the cover of *'Heroes'* comes across as a combination of both works of art. Heckel had given his Kirchner portraits their title after the character in Jean Paul's *Titan*, a highly complex novel which appeared between 1800 and 1803. Heckel reads the book while on the battlefields of Flanders, Roquairol is one of the main characters in this multi-facetted aristocratic story, he is a bon viveur and a Don Juan, not a consistent character but bipolar, one moment a friend, the next an enemy, a *cracked actor* who dies on stage. The image of the 'sensitive Roquairol overflowing with life, whose split personality is, to be sure, striving to do good while being unable to suppress evil', as the catalogue of the Brücke-Museum puts it, can be applied to Kirchner's image, who was at one time a friend of Heckel and then ceased to be. Artistic characters, struggling with their souls, Kirchner was undergoing treatment at the time in Davos suffering from post-traumatic stress following his experiences at the Front, afraid that he is faced with no longer being able to use his hand to paint.

Portrait of the artist Ernst Ludwig Kirchner as a broken man: *Roquairol* by Erich Heckel, painted in 1915, inspiration for the cover of *'Heroes'*.

A singer who chooses not to use his voice, identifies with the portrait of a painter, afraid of losing his most important instrument, Bowie has, it seems, made it easy for people to interpret him as he provides them with so many interpretations of himself. In the same way as he appears to be announcing the solution to most of the riddles he has created, making it crystal clear what he is up to. 'We were all pretty excited about letting people know what went into our work', he says in hindsight, 'that we weren't all trying to be Chuck Berry'. Mostly, Bowie's solutions are extremely convincing, for example the references to the Eastern Bloc in the case of *Low*. Bowie often provides his own interpretation himself, as the cover for *'Heroes'* clearly shows. He is making a reference back to art history, heralding a move forward in the dynamic young art form that is pop music, which is, after all, his main occupation. What we see is Bowie looking at Heckel's portrait of Kirchner, the broken artist, the title of it itself a reference to a cracked actor, thus illustrating in itself the interpretation of its subject. And he identifies himself with it, both the schizophrenia and the method of working being revealed. He attempts to take on the role, to explore, as it were, the costume from the inside and to develop it a bit for his own use. But what he is doing is done without intellectual pretensions, Bowie the school drop-out collecting material from all over the place, behaving like an artist, not like a culture vulture – or a pop critic. He looks at his own work and the work of fellow artists and takes what he needs. And the more he enjoys plundering things, the more successful it is. The more he recognizes that his stage performance always had something Brechtian about it, and now coming to Berlin, he suddenly understands that other artists, long dead by now, shared the same problems as him. There's no reason for him to fall silent because he feels trapped and validated at the same time. No, all he has to do is follow on in their shoes and go where they dared to go. 'I had a plan from when I was eight',

Bowie said to Hanif Kureishi. But perhaps he never made that plan all by himself. Perhaps there is another period living on in him, going up to Bowie's time in Berlin and propelling him into the future.

What does he see in Heckel? Erich Heckel, born in 1883, died 1970, is first a poet, then a painter. When he meets Kirchner in 1904, Heckel bumps into him on his staircase and recites chunks from Nietzsche's *Thus Spake Zarathustra* at him. The following year along with his friend and studio mate Kirchner, and also with Karl Schmidt-Rottluff and Fritz Bleyl, he founds the group of artists known as Die Brücke (The Bridge), joined later by Otto Mueller and Max Pechstein. In Autumn 1911 Heckel goes to Berlin, where his pictures start to become more psychological; he is taken with the city, it pursues him. What then does Bowie see in Heckel and his *Roquairol* and the *Männerbildnis*? A multi-talented person with Nietzschean leanings moves to Berlin in order to carry out work on a more intellectual level, having a friend in a mental hospital whom he paints but in whose portrait he makes reference to the past. It is very unlikely that any of these parallels to him and to Iggy Pop were lost on Bowie. And in general, what unites Die Brücke and its members, all of them students of architecture, is the desire to change the course of things. It's the hope of closing the gap between the different genres of creative art, again something Bowie has been working at since the age of eight. It was Schmidt-Rottluff who is said to have expressed the wish to be a bridge. His death is in August 1976, eleven days before Bowie first sees inside Hansa Studios. 'I became a rock star', Bowie says shortly afterwards. 'It's what I do. It's not my whole life.' When he left Berlin to be hailed as an actor in the role of *The Elephant Man* on the stage in America, he was finally able to proclaim to the world: 'The chauvinism between various art forms – theatre and film, film and music – it's all so silly . . . there is no barrier.'

The dreams of his youth come true. Bowie's Berlin years are taken up with producing an all-round work of art. Isherwood's Schöneberg is the source of this Gesamtkunstwerk but it's a source that is soon exhausted. Bowie himself admits to *Goodbye to Berlin* having been in the end a purely superficial influence. At most the track 'Sons of the Silent Age' on the new album, which he starts work on in July 1977, might be a slight nod towards Brian Roberts and Sally Bowles. The works of Heckel and Kirchner and also of Otto Mueller, on the other hand, influence him in a way that one can only inadequately describe as inspirational. Bowie is not so much inspired by their paintings, as if art could be explained in terms of stimulus and response. Instead, he is more like a double, an aftertaste, a second sight.

There is a scene in Arno Schmidt's 1965 story 'Dark Mirrors' that could well apply to Bowie and Berlin and Bloch, in which the last man on earth, a know-all type of which there are many in Schmidt's writing, is walking through a post-nuclear Germany. Just as in *Diamond Dogs*, where the world has been destroyed but Bowie is still singing his songs, in a similar way this last human being in 'Dark Mirrors' still keeps on writing and quoting. He even takes photographs of himself reading. Finally, and this is the point, he writes a postcard to the writer and poet Klopstock: 'To Herr Klopstock ("Gottlieb or whatever your first name is")', it says. 'Find enclosed *Der Messias* returned.' This is Klopstock's 'heroic poem', *The Messiah*, from 1772. The last human being then pops the card into a postbox from which it will never be collected. Perhaps he does this because he is slowly going mad, or perhaps because any sense of time has become relative in the eternal limbo following a nuclear disaster. But he mainly does it because he believes that, in the indestructible realm of art and its symbols, life still goes on via a parallel existence linking different eras together. 'Everything that has ever been written, in love or hate', Arno Schmidt declares in another of his novels, should be 'treated as still happening live!'

All very well and good, you might be thinking, but what's this got to do with pop music? Does it sound any different just because the guy doing it has got some hobby or other? Bowie is an intelligent guy, okay, he reads books, he occasionally watches films, he paints a bit and goes to museums. Don't hundreds of thousands of people do the same!

It has everything to do with pop music, though. We listen to it differently. Pop music is what makes all these things possible in the first place – and it makes sense of them. It is the only form of art uniting all three dimensions of the creative arts in one. Sound, vision, speech, they all come together in performance. Everything that has ever been written is treated as still happening live. That's Bowie's way of doing it. Or Roxy Music. Or ABC later on. If you are not like Status Quo in their jeans at that time rockin' all over the world, but using the stage as a theatrical space, your own body as a launch pad and the album cover as a caption. No art form involving music, with the exception of opera, ballet and related genres, integrates physical presence and costume in the means of expression to such a degree as pop music. Nobody dances to jazz music anymore, neither the musicians nor the listeners. Chamber orchestras don't normally prance around the stage in fancy dress – nor do the public for that matter. With the help of sound and vision, pop music goes symbolically over the top. It doesn't really have to, but it does, and it's this being so OTT that makes it such a rich experience. And it does everything – this is the surprising thing – in the shortest of time-spans. We learn more from a three minute record (baby) than we ever learn in school, sings Bruce Springsteen. That's who Bowie got his pianist from.

Time and pop music, it's like the postcard to Klopstock. Bowie, dressed like Brecht, singing a number about the Berlin Wall in a video with incredible, state-of-the-art electronic sounds. What date are we talking about then? 1928, 1961, 1977 or later? The present moment for someone listening to 'Heroes' on their stereo is not of any relevance here. To call a pop song something like eclectic, meaning a mishmash of different periods, doesn't do it justice. It blurs the distinctions – this is what makes it – between different eras and genres and for three minutes it brings all influences together in the present. A pop song is the simultaneity of the non-simultaneous performed live.

And it's no coincidence that it is Berlin where Bowie records this sort of historical music. The idea would never have occurred to him in Los Angeles. He clearly needs a backdrop that is made of stone rather than papier mâché. And he finds a spiritual home against one of these backdrops, the Brücke-Museum, a low-key, flat-roof building opened in 1967 with works donated by Heckel and Schmidt-Rottluff. He is a regular visitor there in the Grunewald, certainly more frequently than he goes to the punk clubs in the city – he avoids these clubs because he finds them boring. Nevertheless, Bowie and Iggy Pop turn up at the opening of the legendary punk club SO36 on Oranienstrasse in Kreuzberg. Thomas Schwebel – then with the band Mittagspause, later with Fehlfarben – recalls Bowie roaring up in the Mercedes: 'Bowie looked totally rubbish with his tinted glasses and white suit.' Everyone makes a rush for Bowie, but Iggy disappears to the toilet. Later on Iggy, aka Jim Osterberg, is supposed to have cracked Jewish jokes, 'being an American Jew', Schwebel says: 'The Germans all stood there straight-faced. But they both killed themselves laughing.' It is at SO36 that Iggy Pop once asks Gerrit Meijer from the Berlin band PVC about cocaine. Meijer is horrified. The plan to 'kick drugs in the heroin capital of the world', as Iggy Pop termed it, is clearly not getting very far.

But everything else is. In the meantime we have arrived in the summer of 1977. Up to May, Bowie has accompanied Iggy Pop as keyboard player on his tour with *The Idiot*, then they go straight into Hansa Studios to record *Lust for Life* with the aid of Eduard Meyer, and by the time they have finished it, it's July. Around this time the phone rings in Forst. The receiver is picked up by Michael Rother, who that year achieved great success with *Flammende Herzen*, his solo debut after the demise of Harmonia. There is someone from Bowie's management on the line. David, the voice says, is asking whether Rother fancies making music with him in Berlin, along with Eno too. '*Jawohl*', Rother says straightaway. But he still asks to talk to David in person, so Rother can hear directly from him exactly what he wants.

'Then he called me', Rother still remembers, talking again on the phone from Forst. 'We spoke for a long time and enthusiastically about music and which instruments I should bring along.' Rother suggests Jaki Liebezeit, the drummer from Can, could also join them. 'It was all very positive. We were both very much looking forward to working together on something.'

What they decide to work on together is the album that is later to be called '*Heroes*'. Unlike in the case of *Low* nothing has yet been prepared when he goes into Hansa Studios with his guys. Eno says later that it was exhausting and no easy matter, as all of the songs on the new album only emerged at the mixing desk except for 'Sons of the Silent Age'. Perhaps that's the reason why Bowie makes that call to Forst in the Weser Uplands – to have on hand a musician for once, one whose work is noted for intuition and improvisation – just in case. But it turns out differently, and that is a great shame. An album has gone by the board, its loss a good deal more regrettable than that of the soundtrack of *The Man Who Fell to Earth*.

This is because two or three days later the phone rings again in Forst. 'A new person from the management was on the line', Rother recalls, 'telling me that David had changed his mind and I was no longer needed'. Just like that? 'I was certainly very confused and thought the way I was turned down was just not on. OK, I didn't question it at the time.' Rother chooses his words carefully, whether talking about new music or old tales.

By 'confused' he really means pissed off and offended. But
fortunately he isn't such a big Bowie fan as his former partner
Klaus Dinger. Either way, he soon comes to terms with the
episode and the fact of having been given the cold shoulder.
'In the summer of 1977 I was anyway very busy following the
success of *Flammende Herzen*, besides I was just about to start
on my second album. I didn't give it much thought at the time.'

For decades, however, Michael Rother says his view was that
Bowie abruptly turned him down after a brief flirtation on the
phone. That is, until 2000, when at the same time the old records
of Neu! are being remade and Bowie gives a big interview to the
British music journal *Uncut* about his time in Germany. And in both
cases, asked for a comment, he says: 'In the summer of '76 I called
Michael Rother and asked whether he would be interested in
working with myself and Brian Eno on my new album entitled
"Low". Although enthusiastic Michael had to decline and to this
day I wonder how that trilogy would have been affected by his
input . . . My original top of my wish list for guitar player on
"Low" was Michael Dinger, from Neu!' 'I really had to object',
Rother now says, 'because clearly we had been told two totally
opposite things. He had been told I had changed my mind, and
I had been told the other way round.' So Rother emails New York
giving Bowie his version of the story, that they had phoned and
then later he had been turned down, and above all his name is
Michael Rother, Dinger is the other one. 'So Bowie apologized
profusely, saying "Where is my memory?"'

Who said what to whom on the phone, as if anyone is going
to remember after 30 years. What did actually happen at the time?
'The logic seems to suggest', Rother says, 'that somebody was
concerned about Bowie's career, his freedom to influence the
choice of musicians that inspire him. Perhaps they thought: we
must stop this mad German getting him even more involved in
experimentation. We need to steer clear of that.' This doesn't

sound unlikely, as Bowie had to be careful about his financial situation at the time, at least that's what he said. Either way, this was part of the cautious attitude of his label at the time *Low* was being launched. 'It occurs to me now', Rother suddenly says, 'there was a further conversation with somebody from the management. They wanted to talk to me about money. That was before I was turned down. I was in a state of euphoria because *Flammende Herzen* was selling so well and I said: "The main thing is that the music is good". I am sure that I would have come to a satisfactory agreement with David, it wasn't a matter of money as far as I was concerned. I have never had a manager, even now, I have always seen to the business side of things myself. On the other hand, it probably came across as suspicious. It could be Bowie's management were concerned, thinking: We've got a right hard nut here, first he agrees to something and then he says, OK, if that's the case, you'll have to pay through the nose for it.'

So in July 1977 work begins on *'Heroes'* without Michael Rother. Instead, Eno and Bowie get each other going in Hansa Studio 2 by using the 'Oblique Strategy Cards' that were called upon in the case of *Low*. 'It was like a game', Eno says for example about 'Sense of Doubt', the bleakest track on the new album, again like all the instrumental pieces, on the second side just like *Low*. 'We took turns working on it; he'd do one overdub and I'd do the next. The idea was that each was to observe his Oblique Strategy as closely as he could. And as it turned out they were entirely opposed to one another. Effectively mine said, "Try to make everything as similar as possible" and his said, "Emphasize the differences".' When later they get totally stuck and need a guitar player who can improvise freely and is prepared to go out on a limb without worrying too much about the consequences to his instrument, they call up Robert Fripp.

Then suddenly it all takes off again. Everybody is gobsmacked when Bowie himself falls silent. Now, only a few months later, he starts singing again. He doesn't sing just any old song, though, what he sings is an anthem right away. How it originated has become the stuff of legend, several versions of which are going the rounds. Bowie sings a song whose 'texture' – his favourite word at the time – is so richly woven that it can be used for any type of occasion. The texture is used in the appeal for Africa at the Live Aid concert at London's Wembley Stadium in 1985. It is used in the concert given at New York's Madison Square Garden for the victims of 9/11 six weeks after the terrorist attack. It is even used in advertisements for a brand of sports gear at the Beijing Olympic Games in 2008. The texture can be used because right from the start Bowie puts it in quotation marks. So right from the word go the song is a quotation. And it goes on to have a life of its own, as is always the case with quotations. Just like Ernst Reuter (mayor of West Berlin) said in 1948: 'People of this world . . . look upon this city and see that you should not, cannot abandon this city and this people'. And Walter Ulbricht's (leader of Communist East Germany): 'Nobody has the intention to erect a Wall' (15 June 1961, less than two months before construction began). Or Kennedy's '*Ich bin ein Berliner*'. The texture of this song can be used to refer to all these quotations, as they are what it is about. The song is 'Heroes'.

7 HEROES

Hansa Studios right by the Wall are big. When David Bowie starts
on the recording of *'Heroes'* in the Meistersaal there in July 1977,
right next door the Berlin jazz-rock band Messengers are also
working on new numbers. Their singer is called Antonia Maaß.
She goes on to become part of the myth of Bowie in Berlin as
the woman who did an awful German translation of 'Heroes'.
'Someone called Antonia Maaß', writes Heinz Rudolf Kunze,
'has translated the original in such a ham way that the word
"inept", never normally applied to Bowie, springs to mind.'
It was quite different, Maaß says now, it couldn't be otherwise,
that's what she also explained in great detail to a Berlin
journalist who didn't report it, though. That's why she is upset,
and suspicious. Few witnesses of the period managed to get so
close to Bowie at the time. None of them, however, talk about
him so disaffectedly.

'Like a ray of light', she says now, is how she remembers the
images of the time, the two bands in Hansa Studios, right next
door to one another. The evening in the Eierschale jazz club on
Breitenbachplatz, where Bowie's musicians – Dennis Davis on
drums, Carlos Alomar on guitar, George Murray on bass, in other
words the core group of the Berlin Triptych – go on stage jamming
with the Messengers. The way in which things 'spark' between
her and Tony Visconti. A discreet affair. Long walks along the
Havel river. Nights in her apartment, an *altbau* in Wartburgstrasse,

less than ten minutes away from Bowie's apartment. Bowie, an 'unassuming, small, delicate man', a bit distant, but chummy with his mates. Nothing like one of your high and mighty stars, more a *'primus inter pares'*, according to her.

These are the pleasant memories. Maaß only hints at the unpleasant ones, for example a Berlin concert of Iggy Pop's some time in 1977. Hard, very hard drugs. She is shocked. She doesn't want anything to do with all that. She is 'terribly frightened'. She doesn't even drink alcohol. 'I didn't want to get drawn into it', she says. 'It was like playing with fire as far as I was concerned.' For Visconti, a deeply devoted Buddhist, it was different, which impressed her. And what about Bowie? 'I wasn't drawn to him as a person.' All the same, Maaß, then 33 years old, sings in 'Beauty and the Beast', the first track on the new Bowie album. And she also sings on 'Heroes', in the chorus: 'We can be heroes / Just for one day.'

There are those who say that this song is about Antonia Maaß. And about Visconti. The couple kissing by the Wall, that's you two after all! But that's not the case, says Maaß. When Bowie writes the song, she and Tony are not yet a couple. Besides, they would also both have made sure later on that no one found out about them. Even now she hesitates to mention the name of the man she had an affair with in 1977. Tony Visconti was, after all, married at the time. Still, at least. '(Mary found out)' he writes later in his auto-biography, putting this in brackets. Ashamed. Or glossing over it. Bowie himself does not go along with his producer's relationship, that's what Maaß sensed anyway, even if he doesn't show it in her company. When asked now about the background to 'Heroes', Bowie says, that it's up to Visconti to explain, which he does by saying, 'I can't tell you where he pulled the other images in his song, but we were the couple.' Coco Schwab immediately thought so as well, Visconti says. He sounds a tiny bit proud and ashamed at the same time at this. Maaß, however, says: 'No way was it us.'

Work on the new album takes two months. Bowie is relieved, almost 'happy', he says later. He works very quickly. Mostly Eno, Visconti and him decide on taking the first recording done of a number. Because the second one isn't quite as good. 'Shit', Eno says, who normally agonizes endlessly over the things he is working on, 'it can't be this easy'. Saying this, the conditions in Hansa Studio 2 are far from ideal, or at least a bit tricky, a wall separating the Meistersaal where the musicians play from the control room where the mixing desk is. There is a wall running through the studio next to the Wall, where Bowie writes a song about the Wall. A video camera records what is happening in the large hall on the first floor and relays it to the black-and-white monitor in the Green Room. The equipment is originally from the decaying Hotel Esplanade on Potsdamer Platz, located not very far away. There was a complete film studio installed there which had fallen out of use in the meantime, so Eduard Meyer's former boss bought the equipment, a simple camera that could be moved about in the studio, set up either on a tripod facing the singer or facing the band, in a wide angle. Iggy Pop, according to Meyer, is said to have pulled some great faces at the camera. 'Bowie and Visconti cracked up.' But usually Iggy sits on the windowsill in the kitchen area, doing nothing but writing his lyrics on endless sheets of paper.

Bowie, on the other hand, mostly doesn't know what he is going to sing until he is at the microphone. He has been irritating Visconti now for years by doing this. Bowie is the only one Visconti allows to do this. Bowie writes a few lines, then tries singing them, thinks about it, listens to what they have recorded, adds lines; true, it's very irritating, but on the other hand that way he needs only a couple of hours to write the lyrics for a whole song. Only the title track, according to Visconti, only 'Heroes' was written in the conventional way by Bowie. He sat down, wrote out the verses and the tune and then started singing them.

The new album starts with a quotation from Eno's so-called 'magic briefcase', a portable EMS synthesizer. 'Beauty and the Beast' begins with the noise of sawing. It sounds almost exactly the same as the noise of sawing used by Eno in 1975 on *Another Green World*, likewise on the first track called 'Sky Saw'. 'Art Decade' had similarly referred back to 'Sombre Reptiles' on the same album by Eno, in other words it is not the first time for such a link. 'I don't wish to reproduce what's already been done', Bowie says nevertheless.

> I'd much rather use the synthesizer because there is a texture. And if I need a sound that I haven't heard in my head then I require the assistant at the synthesizer to give me a texture that doesn't exist. If I want a guitar sound I use a real guitar but then I might mistreat it by putting it through the synthesizer afterwards.

We better not look too closely at who might be referred to as 'the assistant at the synthesizer'. In any case Brian Eno has a massive input regarding the new album, so much so that Tony Visconti, even today repeatedly – and feeling somewhat wounded – points out that he was the one who produced *'Heroes'*.

Once again then the album is divided into one side paranoia-rock and another side on which Bowie is silent, this time on only three tracks. Then he starts singing again. The compulsion to keep his mouth shut is clearly wearing off, a sign of return to health perhaps? 'I am not creating narrative-formed albums at the moment', Bowie says at this time, that is to say, he has no need of an alter ego for his Berlin records. Or there again: David Bowie in Berlin is David Bowie, the serious artist working according to a system. 'It started off as experimental work', he says, but I've had such a good time and I developed such enthusiasm for what we are doing that I can see an extension of the way that I'm writing for some time to come until the initial spark of enthusiasm leaves it and then of course I'll move on from there. But at the moment I'm very excited about the process of writing.

Writing. Bowie calls what he is doing writing, not composing. For him it's more like a permanent state rather than a conscious act. He uses the word almost in the sense the French philosopher Roland Barthes uses it, with writing seen as a process in which the writing subject is subsumed, becoming part of the text. There are interviews from this period where the journalists are continually stopping, exasperated, to make sure they have understood properly: You mean writing, Mr Bowie, like writing books? And Bowie provocatively replies, that's *exactly* what he is doing, he is working on a collection of short stories. What he really means by writing, though, is what he has been doing the whole time. Music. And all the rest of it. Here the journalists are, as intended, very impressed by this towering talent explaining his work to them in all modesty.

Artistic types, piss artists, the alternative society of a city with no closing time are the subjects of the first side of *'Heroes'*. The second track, 'Joe the Lion', refers to the American performance artist Chris Burden who had himself nailed to a vw Beetle, Bowie finds him funny even now. 'Blackout', the last track on the first side, falls into the black hole of his marriage breakdown. But like Visconti cheating on his wife, Bowie puts the essential in brackets: 'Get me on my feet (get some direction)', he sings. Bowie seems really to be getting his feet more firmly on the ground. Either way, he has found a new direction, bringing this to a climax by the time of his second Berlin album in the (neurotic, adult) art-rock song for people with taste. Entirely lacking pomposity, gratingly electronic, over the top in a cool sort of way and with lyrics that are more spoken, mumbled even, than sung. Before Bowie, it was The Velvet Underground who introduced this urban neurotic style into pop music. After Bowie, it is Talking Heads from New York who bring it right into the Eighties, likewise with the aid of Eno.

There are 32 tracks in what is called the Berlin Triptych. The name of the city isn't mentioned in a single one of them. If Bowie does ever refer to parts of the city of Berlin, he misspells them. And he does this not just once, but twice even (reminding one of Kunze talking of how 'the word "inept", never normally applied to Bowie, springs to mind'). The first time it happens is in 'Neuköln' (instead of 'Neukölln'), the next-to-last instrumental on *'Heroes'*, which with its atonal, orientalizing saxophone most gives the impression of documentary truth on the new album. It becomes truly embarrassing later, however, when he refers to the area bordering on Neukölln, Kreuzberg, as 'Kreutzburg'. This is what Bowie calls it twenty years later on his 1995 concept album *Outside*, which contains diary entries that many biographers take to be genuine. The printed text is said to be made up of quotations from a diary that Bowie actually kept during his time at 155 Hauptstrasse. This may well be true, he mentions something like that at the time in an interview. 'June 15, 1977, Kreutzburg, Berlin', so that's what Bowie sticks to on *Outside*.

It's two in the morning. I can't sleep for the screaming of some poor ostracised Turkish immigrant screaming his guts out from over the street. His hawking shriek sounds semi-stifled like he's got a pillow over his mouth. But the desperation comes through the spongy rubber like a knife. It cuts the breeze and bangs my eardrums. I take a walk past the fabric machine, turn left onto a street with no name.

From this point the diary writer plunges deeper into the underworld of human experimentation and ritual murders that *Outside* is all about. It is Bowie's first collaboration with Brian Eno for almost twenty years, a very ambitious album that could well have stayed on the drawing board like *Low*. Screaming Turks, human experimentation, is this then what the 'Kreutzburg' nights were like as he lay awake on his mattress in Schöneberg below the portrait of suicide artist Yukio Mishima? Berlin was certainly all around when Eno and Bowie go back into the studio in the mid-'90s. A reference for old times' sake.

The first instrumental on the second side of *'Heroes'* is called 'V-2 Schneider'. It isn't really an instrumental because Bowie repeatedly sings the title on it on the other hand that's all he does. 'V-2 Schneider' is addressed to Kraftwerk's Florian Schneider, whose father built Cologne/Bonn Airport, which, as mentioned, inspired Eno to create *Music for Airports*. Nothing on it, it is true, sounds like Kraftwerk. It's like Bowie always said: he doesn't copy Kraftwerk's cool techno, as it just doesn't fit in with the sort of music he himself makes. 'V-2 Schneider' is more like swing, as though Bowie is turning back into a Mod. With its march-like drum-beat, its saxophone and distorted choral singing the track generally comes across as being not all that serious.

During the Second World War a V-2 rocket had landed near Bowie's grandparents' house in Southborough. The song reduces the world, that is, Germany to a Fleet Street view of things, the stereotypes churned out by British tabloid journalists fighting the war against the Germans all over again, as they were at that time and still even now. Watch out, the Krauts are back, their rockets landing in our front gardens, but not to worry, listen to Vera Lynn singing 'The White Cliffs of Dover', summon up the old Dunkirk spirit and keep a stiff upper lip. The cultural critic Paul Gilroy once said that, in British culture, this always going on about the Nazis was 'so that Brits can know who we are as well as who we were and then become certain that we are still good while our uncivilized enemies are irredeemably evil.' Perhaps Bowie in 'V-2 Schneider' is addressing his comments, not just to Florian Schneider in Düsseldorf, but also directing them at his British critics who call him a Hun-lover just for choosing to go and live in Berlin. There again, perhaps he just likes the way 'V-2 Schneider' sounds.

Sounds are what *'Heroes'* is all about, after all, even more than in the case of *Low*. Bowie tries to tame them and incorporate them into his edgy art rock. Eno, his partner, has after all been dreaming for ages of a kind of music that merges in with the background. The second side of *'Heroes'* comes close to this. Dogs barking. Pipes gurgling. Wind blowing. Planes circling above the city, Tempelhof airport being not that far away from 155 Hauptstrasse. To add to this, Eno and Bowie create a neurotic kind of music using their electronic equipment, more neurotic even than *Low* was, and certainly more chilly. Sickly. As cold as the grave. Bowie has removed all colour from the images, in an eternal Berlin November. 'Neuköln' and particularly 'Sense of Doubt' on this forlorn second side of *'Heroes'* come across as made for a film that hasn't yet been shot, but it is in the process of being, called 'Germany in Autumn'.

In fact, 'Sense of Doubt' is used four years later in Ulrich Edel's film *Wir Kinder vom Bahnhof Zoo* (*We Children from Bahnhof Zoo*), the notes on the piano accompanying the listener down an escalator, banging hard, footsteps echoing loudly. We're on our way down into Kurfürstendamm underground station, where the hoards of pale-faced kids on the drug scene hang out, or going into the tunnel on Line 1 at Gleisdreieck station. The icy synthesizer blasts of 'Sense of Doubt' set the scene in the film equally well for Kantstrasse as for the toilets in Zoo station. Or where under-age hookers work Kurfürstenstrasse, Christiane F. gets into a client's car, as it's making a turn, we catch a glimpse

briefly in the distance of the kind of *altbau* facades that Wolf Jobst
Siedler reproduced in *Die gemordete Stadt* (*The Murdered City*).
Anyone who has seen how well 'Sense of Doubt' accompanies
Edel's images for the machines for living in, the ugly face of West
Berlin, how well the track sets to music the decay, horror and the
'*einstürzende Neubauten*', the crumbling new buildings, can see
why at the time Christiane F. considers Bowie's music to be the
soundtrack of her life.

'Neukölln', on the other hand, this kebab shop version of
ambient music, reminds Eno most of all of the fading imagery
of Die Brücke. Visconti's favourite track, though, is 'Moss
Garden'. Perhaps because the producer is a practising Buddhist.
On it Bowie plucks at a koto, a Japanese zither. This track exudes
a lulling quality, suddenly turning the harshness into a gentle,
soothing lullaby. Tension is released, calm returns, and we get a
hint of happiness. There is no other track from Bowie's time in
Berlin that sounds quite like this 'Moss Garden'. It seems like an
island marooned in the middle of '*Heroes*', surrounded as it is by
the border restricted area. Only the dogs occasionally barking in
the course of the five minutes and the planes circling overhead
remind you of what is lying in wait beyond the garden: no man's
land. 'Very sloppy sort of technique', Eno says about the way
he and Bowie produce 'Moss Garden'. 'I was just playing around
with this chord sequence on the Yamaha synthesiser and I said
"Give us a shout when you think it's long enough" . . . and then
David looked at the clock and said "Yeah, that'll probably do",
and we stopped.' Perhaps Bowie looked at the clock and saw
that the Brücke-Museum was closing soon. His music and the
museums – that's all Bowie is interested in regarding Berlin,
Antonia Maaß claims.

Towards the end, in the course of the last three tracks, the
compass needle on '*Heroes*' swings back and forth between the
Middle and the Far East. Bonsai in a Japanese garden, that's

what 'Moss Garden' sounds like. An Oriental saxophone on the Hermannplatz, that's what 'Neuköln' sounds like. Finally the track 'The Secret Life of Arabia', on which the guitar weaves about in almost Maghrebi style as though Carlos Alomar is playing on the many-stringed oud. The track is totally exceptional, Bowie suddenly turning into Lawrence of Arabia. He even looks a bit like Peter O'Toole, the actor who would probably have played the role of *The Man Who Fell to Earth* if Nicolas Roeg hadn't seen Bowie on television. Above all, though, 'The Secret Life of Arabia' is a beacon pointing towards the next phase. 'It's often struck me', Bowie says, 'that there will usually be one track on any given album of mine, which will be a fair indicator of the intent of the following album.' The title track of *Station to Station* preempts the claustrophobia of *Low*, the second silent side of that album basically forming a link to *'Heroes'*. Finally, on *'Heroes'* this ethno-rock 'Secret Life of Arabia' looks forward to *Lodger*, the last part of the Berlin Triptych' – World Music. That's Bowie's next phase. Great men, journeys, adventure. Perhaps we have Berlin with its Wall to thank for turning Bowie into an ethnographer. Islands are famous for having a variety of species. But before he can finally open his music up to the world, Bowie first has to sing about the border itself.

All great songs start small. One afternoon in the summer of 1977 Visconti, Bowie and Eno are playing around with a sequence of chords that Bowie and Eno have worked out together, producing eight minutes of material, a song without a name. And these eight minutes turn into seven days that Eno spends putting together the tracks of the song without name they have been working on.

It's not a bad song, but there's something still missing for it to become a really good song, unforgettably good. It lacks a guitar. Bowie grabs the phone and dials a number. But he isn't phoning Michael Rother in the Weser Uplands but rather Robert Fripp in New York. Eno has already worked twice with the guitarist for

King Crimson, a British specialist band that broke up two years before and whose brand of progressive art rock already enjoys a legendary reputation. Eno and Fripp had already played around with tape machines on *Evening Star* and *No Pussyfooting*, creating sound loops, the two of them calling their home-made technique 'Frippertronics'. Everything guys like Eno and Fripp attempt at the time in the studio by way of experiment is cobbled together. They are breaking new ground whatever they do because there is still, for example, no digital storage making it easy for them to delay and manipulate sounds and tracks. They create bridges by hand, unwinding metre after metre of tape in the studio. They measure the time by stopwatch and press buttons, and if what they are recording gets out of sync, they have to throw away the tape and start again from scratch. Trial and error, Visconti says, is what these early days in Berlin consist of. 'I thrive on mistakes', Bowie says. 'If I haven't made three good mistakes a week, then I'm not worth anything.'

So the phone rings in New York, and Fripp answers. 'Do you think you could play some hoary rock 'n' roll?' Bowie is supposed to have asked. And so Fripp grabs the next plane to Europe, lands in West Berlin, goes to Hansa Studios, doesn't even listen to the song he was summoned for but just plugs the guitar he has brought with him into the effects processor, links it up to Eno's synthesizer, places himself in front of the amplifiers ready to feed in – and away he goes. A riff. Three long drawn-out notes, and the rest is history.

That's how the myth goes anyway. It sounds too good to be true. Fripp drops everything on a whim, packs his guitar and luggage (just like Visconti and the Harmonizer), flies halfway across the world with nothing better to do than play straight off a tune that has even now lost none of its sense of yearning, its bittersweet quality and its brilliance. Fripp stays only a couple of days at Hansa Studios, not playing on all the tracks, but without

Fripp's overstrained, multi-dimensional guitar the new album
would not sound half as deliciously shattered, desolate and great.

The riff that Fripp is said to have written still more or less
jet-lagged, is further mistreated by Eno using his equipment. He
extends, stretches and lengthens it, unfolds it, massages it – or
whatever he does fiddling with the buttons and controls of his
magic briefcase, aimed at robbing the sound of the guitar of the
last traces of hoary rock 'n' roll. He fiddles with it until there is
nothing identifiably conventional left. 'What does the human soul
look like?' is the question put by the magazine *Titanic* some years
ago in one of its series, asking for contributions from readers –
this at least could be one way of listening to the soul, a deeply
human sound, slowly fading, picking up again, then fading again.
The four of them in the studio record three versions of the track,
as if they couldn't get enough of it. And when Visconti eventually
puts these three tracks together, playing them simultaneously, the
musical texture of 'Heroes' is complete.

Just how strong it is without lyrics becomes evident whenever
Bowie plays the number live. Fripp's riff, it's true, often comes
across on stage as one-dimensional, less substantial than on the
album, thin somehow; it's clearly not enough for this tune to be
only played on one guitar. What Eno and Visconti create in the
studio process, these thousands of undertones, background
noises, branching off in all directions, this whole wall of sound
is simply lacking in that case. As regards the sound, 'Heroes' is
already in 1977 what is called in the 1980s 'Noise' and in the '90s
'Shoegaze', a highly sensitive, mournful, marvellous din, no solo
guitar, no musicians showing off, no rock hierarchy looking down
their noses. A finely interwoven collective noise to the sobbing of
thin young boys – and Bowie is *the* thin young boy – revealing the
secrets of their diaries to the mike.

Heroes at work: Robert Fripp, Brian Eno and Bowie in the Meistersaal at Hansa Studios
in 1977.

But there are as yet no lyrics to the song without a name.
So Bowie throws everybody out so he can write them. When it's
ready, Visconti sets up three microphones in the Meistersaal, the
first one right in front of Bowie's nose, the next one six and the
last fifteen metres away from him. One by one he turns them on
so as to catch the full epic range of Bowie going from a whisper
to a shout. Visconti now talks of this having a 'Wagnerian'
passion, but this is as ridiculous as saying that Low is Hun music.
It's just that Bowie has to pull out all the stops on this occasion,
that's what makes it so passionate.

The Wall has been up for sixteen years when in the summer
of 1977 Bowie writes 'Heroes'. But in the course of these sixteen
years and the 30 or so years since, nobody else has dared to write
another such emotional song about the Wall. Maybe someone
has in the privacy of their own four walls. 'Heroes', however, is
still today the only pop song that has achieved worldwide fame
because of it. And it has become a bit more famous on every
occasion that its title has been cashed in on as a catchphrase in
front of millions of the public, by Bowie and others who have
paid for it: we can be heroes and end hunger in Ethiopia. We
can be heroes and buy this computer program. We can be heroes
and bury the dead of 9/11. We can be heroes and win gold, at the
Winter Olympics in Nagano, at the Summer Games in Beijing.
None of this has done any harm to the song that Bowie writes
at the window in Hansa Studios.

Whatever Bowie sees on the day he throws his crew out to
write his lyrics, it all starts with a view. The myth has fed on this
image, Tony Visconti having put it in his autobiography a few
years back. Bowie, in his green-check garage mechanic's shirt
and with his 'tash, there he is, sitting in the control room of
Hansa Studio 2, smoking a Gitanes, with his hand against his
head, thinking. On the left-hand wall is the monitor from the
Esplanade, on which you can dimly make out the mike stands

and amplifiers. Of the music that Bowie records in the Meistersaal, the first thing he sees are electronic images, and they are in black and white, like old-fashioned pictures always are; perhaps that's the reason the cover of *'Heroes'* is black and white. Either way, to the right of Bowie as he is smoking and lost in thought there is a window, outside a dark-blue Berlin sky, is that a border guard you can see there by the Wall? Visconti's caption to this image is that Bowie can be seen writing the lyrics for 'Heroes'.

But that would mean that Visconti – if he took the photo himself and can even produce evidence for what he claims – realized the importance of that moment and that's why he pressed the button. Wasn't Bowie supposed to be all on his own in the studio while he was writing? This is being picky, after all, Visconti's description of the photo is probably only a figment of his imagination. It would be nice for the story of the image to be true. Nevertheless it is still strange that, of all people, level-headed Eno, getting increasingly wound up towards the end of the project, is the one who says that, fiddling around with the new song without a name, 'I had that very word – heroes – in mind', as the song sounded so grand and heroic. And when Bowie played the finished album to him, he couldn't believe it. What a case of déjà vu! He finds it quite uncanny.

So 'Heroes' starts with a view. Not a view of the monitor in Studio 2 but out of the window next to him, down the street, in the direction of the Wall, 200 metres from Bowie's chair at the control desk.

Everything Bowie in his own right says about the origin should be put in quotation marks just as he does with the whole track of 'Heroes'. Using inverted commas provides a certain amount of detachment, keeps the real world at bay. Visconti has bracketed the embarrassing revelation of his affair with Antonia Maaß, Bowie simply glosses over the boundless idealism of his song called 'Heroes' by being ironic about it right from the start.

Issuing an artful warning: be careful, from now on what I say is not for real. *Achtung*, you are entering the irony-occupied sector. Heinz Rudolf Kunze imagines that Bowie felt upstaged by The Stranglers with their new album *No More Heroes* beating him to it, but he didn't want to come across as an aging rocker still hooked on what the young punks have been taking the piss out of already. There are just four weeks between the release of both albums. It is doubtful whether Bowie would really have made such a fuss just to ward off competition, something he doesn't give a toss about anyway. That at least is what he says.

The scene he claims to have witnessed, Bowie shared with the same pop journalist from the NME who barely six months before had written the most scathing critique ever of *Low* – Charles Shaar Murray. 'The situation that sparked off the whole thing was – I thought – highly ironic', is what Bowie tells him in November 1977. There's a wall by the studio, the album having been recorded at Hansa by the Wall in West Berlin.' Not *the*, but *a* wall?

It's about twenty or thirty metres away from the studio and the control room looks out onto it. There's a turret on top of the wall where the guards sit and during the course of lunch break every day, a boy and girl would meet out there and carry on. They were obviously having an affair. And I thought of all the places to meet in Berlin, why pick a bench underneath a guard turret on the Wall?

Of all the places in all the world where you could get back to health, become clean and record music, why is it Berlin Bowie chooses?

Later to another journalist Bowie says he presumed that the couple, aged somewhere around nineteen or twenty, were feeling guilty and took refuge in the shadow of the Wall 'to cause the affair to be an act of heroism. It seemed a very '70s incident and

theme. Personal survival by self-rule.' He finds another, more
telling way of putting it, that 'Heroes' is about 'facing that kind
of reality and standing up to it' so as to 'get on with life from the
very simple pleasure of remaining alive'. And this is equally true
of this song as it is of his time in Berlin. In the few lines at the
end he is again after all only speaking about himself, about having
managed to pull himself up by his own bootstraps from a dark
place. It's about brinkmanship. And about the advantage of turning
the private into the political by merging the Cold War and a love
affair reflecting the traditional ballad of the lovers separated by
the waters of a river unable to get together, in the German version
two 'Königskinder', kings' children.

The lyrics of 'Heroes' lose a lot without its interpreter. He starts
singing the first lines softly, then gets louder and louder, more and
more forthright, right to the end – that's where Visconti turned
all three microphones on full – his voice practically breaking.

Eduard Meyer has nothing to say as to who the couple are
that Bowie is singing about. He only occasionally drops in at
Studio 2 at the time *'Heroes'* is being recorded. Antonia Maaß is
certain: 'It wasn't us in any case!' Because she and Visconti still
weren't involved with one another when the song was created,
that didn't happen until the evening together in the Eierschale,
not until after she had been the backing singer on the album.
And even if it was them, they would never have kissed and
cuddled in public as she wanted to keep their liaison a secret.

But why should there be a couple at all, in a song its creator
intended to be a quotation? The answer to this is again to be
found in the Brücke-Museum. There is a picture by Otto Mueller
called *Lovers between Garden Walls*, painted in 1916 on the Western
Front. Mueller is best known for his girls bathing among the
reeds, dating from shortly after the War. By the time he joins his
friends Heckel and Kirchner in 1910, he has been living in Berlin

One of the images relating to 'Heroes': Otto Mueller's *Lovers between Garden Walls*, painted in 1916.

for some time already. Mueller is ten years older than the others in the Dresden group of artists, born in 1874, and he also dies before the others, in 1930. He volunteers for the First World War, serving first in Flanders and then in France. Irritated by the chatter of his fellow soldiers, horrified by what he has to witness with his own eyes in the trenches, he seeks refuge in art. He paints couples, lots of couples, in bed and in the open air. They embody what he calls in the title of one of his pictures his 'yearning for peace'. Finally in the year of the Battle of Verdun he paints *Lovers between Garden Walls*. A man and a woman in an embrace, not much more than outlined sketches in front of head-high walls that are distorted and white. The two of them are hedged in by stones, reflected in the warm colours surrounding them. It's an elegiac image, it's no surprise Mueller finds solace in such motifs. He has no need of friends to console him at the Front, they talk too much for his liking, all he needs is art. And Bowie, who must have found this all very familiar, who, as he once said, very much identified with the atmosphere of the paintings of Die Brücke, may well have seen any old couple out of the corner of his eye on the Köthener Strasse, a chance encounter in front of a white wall so that the two images merge into one. This could have been like in *The Man Who Fell to Earth*, a kind of double exposure made up of then and now. Bowie, at that time ambitious, writing and painting and singing and acting, striving to become a Renaissance man – this way of interpreting things sounds more feasible than the tabloid press simply putting two and two together. Who was there with whom? The only two things, Eduard Meyer says, all the journalists wanted to know from him was: who were the couple? And was Bowie in bed with Romy Haag? Meyer isn't able to answer either of these questions. They are trivial anyway.

When Bowie looks out of the studio window, he can see the Wall as it is in 1977, and beyond it the waste ground of Potsdamer Platz, surrounded by watchtowers. When Mueller and Heckel and Kirchner come to Berlin, this is the pulsating heart of Berlin teeming with traffic, people, horse-drawn carriages, trams, a bustling, noisy place that is the height of modernity in a city that is forever growing. When Bowie comes here nearly 70 years later, the Platz is no more, its arteries dried up. Running through it is the Wall, that has to wait another thirteen years before it starts to crumble, and eventually fall. And the following year, 1990, Roger Waters makes use of the giant stage that suddenly appears in no-man's-land to perform *The Wall*, the so-called 'rock opera' laden with meaning, with his band Pink Floyd. It's about a star who puts on body armour, who builds a wall around himself. It is executed on a *Diamond Dogs* scale, in July 1990, in front of 200,000 people who find all this highly symbolic. There is room even for such overblown psychological stuff in Bloch's hollow Berlin.

Nowadays it seems a bit like Berlin was only waiting for a
song like 'Heroes'. To Visconti and Bowie themselves it must
have felt like that, a need, perhaps even an opportunity. Either
way, one day the idea spontaneously arises of singing a German
version of 'Heroes'. Visconti calls on his girlfriend, Antonia Maaß.
She's the one to translate the lyrics. Bowie is in Blonay, not in
Berlin, so Maaß travels there. Gloomy memories. One can feel
that she doesn't like to talk about it. 'It was just like living in an
orgy', is all she says about the state of affairs at the chalet. 'I
wanted to get away as quickly as possible from Switzerland.'
That's why she was never bothered about royalties. 'I translated
the lyrics', she says firmly, 'beyond that I didn't want anything to
do with Bowie. I was against getting to know anything else about
him.' But she tries hard to teach him German lyrics that he can
get by with.

'I had to make allowances for Bowie', Maaß says. 'Otherwise
nobody would ever have understood it.' The two of them go
through the lyrics sentence by sentence in the private studio in
Blonay, but Bowie has trouble all the time with the pronunciation,
so Maaß plays around with every line, changing words, until
Bowie no longer stumbles over them and the new lyrics still bear
some relation to the original. She is perfectly aware that some of
the lyrics are not correct German, but Bowie obviously can't get
his mouth round a better translation. He is apparently supposed
to have once ordered steak, roast potatoes and a glass of milk in
broken German at the Café Wien in Berlin, with a journalist from
Rolling Stone there at the time, noting it, rather impressed. But if
you listen to Bowie singing 'Heroes' using the lines Maaß adapted
for him, you begin to wonder what the waiter brought him.

'*Ish bin ine bear-LEAN-ar*' is literally what was written on the
note John F. Kennedy read from on the balcony of Schöneberg
Town Hall in July 1963. '*Ich bin ein Berliner*' is of course what it was
meant to be. Kennedy bequeathed these four words to Berliners

walled up in their city, David Bowie bequeathed an anthem. But
in order that this anthem could be understood by his neighbours,
who call him 'Boffie', Bowie sang it a second time in German
phonetics, just as Kennedy had done. In fact it would have been
enough for Maaß to have translated 'Heroes' using these syllables:
Ish bin ine bear-LEAN-ar.

The attraction that Bowie falls prey to is the same attraction
all American presidents since Kennedy have. They all want to be
a Berliner, an inhabitant of this symbolic city. Ronald Reagan too
speaks in German, giving a speech at the Brandenburg Gate on 12
June 1987: *'Ich habe noch einen Koffer in Berlin'* ('I still have a suitcase
in Berlin'), he says for example, and *'Es gibt nur ein Berlin'* ('There
is only *one* Berlin'). Of course, the Berliners cheer him on the
rostrum every time. Reagan's speech has become famous, because
in it he calls on the Soviet leader Gorbachev to open the
Brandenburg Gate and tear down the Wall if he is really serious
about glasnost and perestroika. There are veterans of the Cold
War who say Reagan's speech was the first hammer blow against
the Wall, which soon starts to crumble, the beginning of the end
as it were. It is much more significant, however, that behind the
President's back, beyond the Brandenburg Gate, in the days just
before this state visit thousands of young people gathered to
protest. It wasn't the American president's visit that drew them
but pop music. The events begin on 6 June and last for three
evenings. They were set off by a concert on the green in front
of the Reichstag. On stage is David Bowie.

It's the day before Whitsunday. Almost exactly ten years
to the day since he went into Hansa Studios to record *'Heroes'*,
Bowie performs in front of the Reichstag. It's the first 'Concert
for Berlin' on the occasion of the 750th anniversary of the
foundation of the city; New Model Army are on before him.
In the course of the day he has been back to Köthener Strasse
and has even had a brief word with Eduard Meyer, there being

of course a historic picture of this reunion. At a press conference
in the studios he says how dismayed he is to see a Wall still out
of the window. Then he goes by taxi to 155 Hauptstrasse, takes
a few photos, but doesn't go into his old apartment building.
In the evening he is on stage in front of the Reichstag. He has
70,000 people at his feet listening to him as he reads a message
in German: '*Wir schicken unsere besten Wünsche an all unsere Freunde,
die auf der anderen Seite der Mauer sind*' ('We send our best wishes
to all our friends who are on the other side of the Wall'). Then he
sings 'Heroes'.

On the other side of the Wall, as close as possible to the
Reichstag, there are hundreds of young East Berliners listening
along to the concert as it echoes across, gathering together in the
Grotewohl-Strasse, by the Charité Hospital and in the Neustädter
Kirchstrasse. They are even sitting on the roofs. Then suddenly
they hear Bowie greeting them. And they hear his song. Their
song. Soon they are charging towards the Brandenburg Gate.
That's where, as the Stasi know, the barriers are very low, you
can easily get into the border restricted area. The Vopo and the
border guards of the NVA, the 'National People's Army', block
the rush. Rocks come flying through the air.

On the following two evenings of the Whitsun weekend when
The Eurythmics and finally Genesis do their 'Concert for Berlin',
the crowds swell in East Berlin, the rioting getting more violent.
The Stasi note in the internal closing report of their Central
Operations' Staff that the situation is becoming more critical
every night. Blockades are set up, a total of '158 persons arrested.
Mainly young adults born between 1964 and 1969. 25 young girls
were arrested. They showed partly aggressive behaviour.' And
like Bowie and Visconti, the Stasi like to put the really essential
thing in brackets and inverted commas: 'The actions of the
People's Police were loudly greeted by whistling and chanting
(*Mauer weg!* – "Down with the Wall")', is how the events of

On 6 June 1987 Bowie returns to Hansa Studios and meets his *Tonmeister* Eduard Meyer. The same evening he performs in front of the Reichstag.

7 June are described. The newspaper *Bild* says it has heard the chant in brackets once already. In the evening Bowie plays 'Heroes'.

(*Mauer weg!*) The youth of East Berlin had last demanded this just as forcefully, courageously and at the tops of their voices on the Alexanderplatz on 7 October 1977, the very week before Bowie released '*Heroes*'. At that time as well, a rock concert sparked off serious riots, hundreds of people being arrested. Fans of FC Union Berlin yelled 'United!', a policeman was said to have been chased across the square minus his clothes. There are unconfirmed reports of three dead, including two Vopo. In the summer ten years later, once again on the streets of East Berlin something is happening that soon is going to be unstoppable, people are becoming restless, more and more noise is being heard in the capital of the GDR. 'The gathering of young people were largely of decadent appearance', the Stasi report on the situation says. 'A sound level check on 8.6 at the Charité Hospital indicated a considerable exceeding of the prescribed limit. Taking account of the fact that in the vicinity of the Charité Hospital there is above all a need for silence.' No way is it going to be deathly silent any more. 'Pigs!', 'Down with the Wall!', 'Russians Out!', is what the decadent mob are shouting. The Wall lasts for another two years. That June East Berlin already saw a few of the heroes that were soon to bring it crashing down.

8 GOODBYE TO BERLIN

An artist who feels at home in Switzerland and America moves into an empty apartment in Schöneberg. It's the 1970s, and the artist is recording what he sees around him. 'Why not describe the streets in this half Berlin, its taverns, its half-share of the Wannsee lake, its pine trees beneath the northern sky?' he notes. 'The apartment lies along the approach path to Tempelhof airport; the planes come over low, making everything in the back yard vibrate, touching down from the west and taking off towards the west; between times silence.' He makes himself temporarily at home. 'The first room to become habitable is the kitchen with its gas stove. The apartment must not be too full of furniture. I think so too, but one does need chairs. The telephone stands on the parquet floor.' He prefers to eat out: 'Oswald Wiener runs a bar called EXIL to which we enjoy going.' He enjoys himself, too, more or less, he likes Scharoun's new building on Potsdamer Platz and above all his new apartment: 'The empty white rooms echo. Music from the little transistor.' This is just the sort of apartment, the artist writes, he has sought in vain in the past: 'Plain, but with high ceilings. And so we have come to Berlin. There are plenty of other reasons: to live together with the Wall, a few friends already there.'

This isn't David Bowie. But it could be: Berlin, the divided city, attracts lots of other artists after all, struggling with identity problems in their work. The one speaking here is Max Frisch. The

Swiss writer described his move to Friedenau, the better end of
Schöneberg, to 8 Sarrazinstrasse (another landmark in Berlin)
in his autobiographical book *Montauk*. A work consisting of
sketches, noted very casually and wearily, appearing in the year
Bowie's longing for Berlin slowly takes off, 1975.

When you start to go through everything that has ever been
written, filmed and sung about Berlin and has gone on treating
it as happening live, you keep coming across connections with
Bowie. So everything is connected with everything else, because
everyone who moves to Berlin on purpose and with ambition
thinks the city must have some connection with them, otherwise
they wouldn't be there. The city is the medium. *Ich und die Stadt*
('The City and Me') is what the Expressionist Ludwig Meidner
called a famous-infamous picture of 1913 identifying himself
forcefully with Berlin, 'mad on the city' is what Meidner himself
would say. The painting shows a torn, urban landscape with
Meidner's likeness in the middle of it. Buildings and streets shoot
out of his artist's moustache, the cracks of his face merging into
stone: 'I Am the City', would have been a better title for Meidner
to give it. There is no longer any difference between the interior
and the exterior, everything is identical, the human being and
walls growing into one another. When Bowie returns to Berlin
for the 750th commemoration and sings 'Heroes' at the Reichstag,
there is one of those blockbuster exhibitions on at the Gropius-Bau
devoted to Meidner's picture and those of his contemporaries on
which Berlin has based its reputation for some time.

Artists in Berlin, united by a common urban experience, only
becoming unified by writing, talking or painting about it. The
very fact that Frisch in 1978 is finishing a work called *Tryptichon*,
just as Bowie the same year is finishing his Berlin Triptych is just
an amazing coincidence. More interesting is the fact that Frisch's
lifelong subject matter is isolation and the search for identity giving
rise to the Berlin passages of *Montauk* being reminiscent of scenes

in Bowie's songs: 'One afternoon by the Schlachtensee; when you are cheerful, I forget again for a while your unhappiness with me.' – 'You're such a wonderful person / but you got problems', is what Bowie sings. It isn't the Schlachtensee he walks by but the Wannsee where he eats *pâté de foie* in gloomy restaurants, if he hasn't booked a table at Ossi Wiener's Exil in Kreuzberg.

'I try on stories like clothes', Max Frisch writes in *Montauk*. Bowie tries on clothes like stories: a Martian hermaphrodite, a dilettante from Mitteleuropa, a Berlin neo-Expressionist. You need to juxtapose the images. If all you see is a city of stage sets and the images reflected on them by the people living there, the images need to be juxtaposed to be made out properly. They are framed by the ever-changing shape of Berlin in which the lives of its inhabitants are bound up inseparably. Everything in it suddenly becomes all the more significant. 'All my life', the British writer G. K. Chesterton wrote, 'I have loved frames and limits; and I will maintain that the largest wilderness looks larger seen through a window.' At the Dschungel on Winterfeldtplatz Bowie is a regular and gives the bar cult status. Out of a window at Hansa Studios he sees a couple by the Wall and turns this scene into a legend.

Even today Berlin is the expat capital, those keen to add a cool address to their cvs. That's what it is for Bowie too, in those three short years. For people like him who have moved to the city from wherever, Berlin is creative for identity, the extension of one's own personality. Finding the right part of town is like going in search of self-identification. Many bands have followed in Bowie's footsteps to Hansa Studios in Berlin, Depeche Mode came at the start of the '80s. Just after the fall of the Berlin Wall it's the turn of the Irish group U2. They had already worked with Brian Eno, and now at Hansa Studios they try to slip into the frame previously occupied by Bowie. What comes of all this? The result in their case is the cod-German *Achtung Baby* – that's the title of their Berlin album, a quotation from *The Producers*, Mel Brooks's musical about the Nazis. The result is also one of those little East German cars called the 'Trabi', the Trabant, being decorated by the Wall graffiti artist Thierry Noir featured on the record's cover. The result is the video of the song 'One', showing the Meistersaal, the Wall and a plush rented room with the members of U2 taking turns sitting on the sofa in drag. Here they are taking in three scenes from Bowie's Berlin, starting with Isherwood's Kit-Kat Club going via Hansa Studios right up to 'Heroes'.

The quest in search of Bowie, the searcher, has over time taken on mythical status, becoming an essential part of the city tours, including seeing the window in Hansa Studios with the view of a blank wall. In the meantime this quotation of a quotation has turned into a parody of itself. In 2008 the Canadian band Stars filmed an amusing video for their number 'Bitches in Tokyo', showing a group of schoolkids starting a glam rock band in a living room, much to the irritation of their parents, the neighbours and the police. Just before they are chucked out, a guy in a tour bus rescues them, he's an impresario in the mould of Malcolm McLaren, who gives his protégées with their make-up and done hair some wise advice about a rock star life style. The most important being: 'You have to threaten or promise endlessly that you are going to move to Berlin.' 'Right, yeah!', the band shout. 'Okay, can everybody say that?' McLaren asks, 'Where are you moving to?' 'Berlin', the first one replies. 'Where are you going next week?' 'Berlin!', the second one shouts and then the third until finally all of them are shouting 'Berlin!!!' For Bowie too, Berlin was the destination for the dreams of his youth.

In October 1977 when Bowie releases 'Heroes', his label RCA finds a new way of describing their difficult artist: 'There's old wave, there's new wave, and there is David Bowie.' And they invent another, no less catchy, slogan with 'Tomorrow belongs to those who can hear it coming.'

A few months before, Bowie didn't even appear in public to advertise *Low*. No promotion, no interviews. This time, however, only nine months later, Bowie goes on television to present the latest music even before the accompanying album has been launched. On 9 September he appears on Marc Bolan's television show singing 'Heroes', a week before Bolan is killed in London in an accident in his Mini Cooper. On 11 September Bowie takes part in a Christmas special with Bing Crosby made by for America's CBS network. It is also Crosby's last TV appearance, his death coming on 14 October, the day *'Heroes'* is released. Two shows, two deaths. Suddenly the two appearances acquire an air of doom, a total coincidence looking like a matter of fate.

Bowie's appearance on the Crosby show would have been remarkable in any case. Simply for the fact that Bowie sings a medley of 'Peace on Earth' and 'Little Drummer Boy' with this great Hollywood star. Even more of a surprise is how Bowie comes across as totally normal. In the acted-out scene of the 'Merrie Olde Christmas TV Show' broadcast on 30 November, he rings the doorbell, Crosby opens the door, and Bowie, in a respectable jacket and wearing a scarf, comes in saying 'I'm David Bowie, I live down the road', and asks whether he can play a bit of piano. The two of them go over to the grand piano and fiddle with a score, Bowie talks about his six-year-old son, about the festive season in the Bowie family, their presents, their Christmas tree and their decorations, finally singing their Christmas medley, followed by Bowie with 'Heroes'. He comes across the whole time as being a totally down-to-earth guy. Crosby asked him for his phone number after the show.

Radio, TV, magazines. Interview after interview. Almost all of his deeper thoughts, statements, ideas and explanations of his move to Berlin go back to this Autumn of 1977. Bowie sings 'Heroes' on German TV, in the Netherlands, on the BBC's 'Top of the Pops' and in France. The gloomy video in which he appears

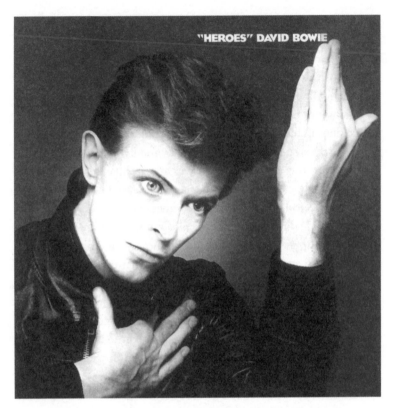

The second part of the Berlin Triptych: *'Heroes'* is released on 14 October 1977.

swathed in clouds of mist and dressed in leather à la Brecht is also filmed at this time by Stanley Dorfman. In Crosby's Christmas show Bowie sings 'Heroes' likewise dressed in jet black, and he goes in for a bit of mime in the way he got from Lindsay Kemp, feeling his way along an invisible wall, pressing an invisible partner to himself, turning his back on the audience and embracing himself. The song, after all, is all about ego. Two videos are made at this time to go with 'Sense of Doubt'. In the first of these, produced by Bowie for the Italian TV show 'Odeon', he is standing at a grand piano in a studio that is probably meant to be the Hansa Meistersaal. Bowie plays the steeply descending piano tune, looking thoughtfully over and over again at the technicians behind the glass partition as they sit in silence at their mixing desk. It comes over as a scene in a laboratory and that's what it is supposed to do. Bowie looks brilliant, even though prancing about rather self-importantly, moving back and forth between the piano and the synthesizer. He is clearly enjoying having all eyes looking with wonder at this guy who is turning away from the conventions of pop music at the peak of his fame. That's why he moves his fingers deliberately: hey, just look how when I press this button here, what comes out is great, serious art.

The second video of 'Sense of Doubt' mainly shows nothing but his hand. Again, music director Dorfman produced it; it clearly originates on the same day of filming as 'Heroes'. Bowie has now only zipped up his black leather jacket. This is so as to be in the spirit of the cover of *'Heroes'*, of Heckel's *Roquairol*, not to mention Ernst Ludwig Kirchner. The camera closes in on the back of his left hand. It remains motionless for a time until Bowie turns his hand over and puts it up to his head, hovering there as on the album cover – then the camera zooms in on Bowie's eyes. It follows Bowie as he makes this movement several times in a row, until finally it draws back and he appears in a medium-long shot, both hands gently clasped on his chest.

It is not the first time Bowie brings a painting to life. Making his debut in front of the camera in Michael Armstrong's 14-minute film *The Image* as early as 1967, he played the subject of a picture knocking at the door of the studio in order to haunt his creator. This silent B-movie is a black-and-white horror film. Over and over again the painter tries to kill his picture that has learned to walk, throwing it downstairs and stabbing it, all to no avail. In the end despite all this, his 'image' is standing back at the easel on which it is being painted, miming the pose on the canvas – hands clasped in an appeal for an embrace.

The film comes over as a sort of poor man's version of *The Picture of Dorian Gray*, but there is a clear line connecting this homoerotic artist's nightmare in which dramatically paint drips from an erect painting brush, to the life of Ziggy Stardust himself through to Heckel's *Roquairol*, a portrait that must have seemed to Bowie like an exposé of his inner-directed world of images. Now in the video Bowie runs into the contorted arms of Heckel's *Roquairol*, empathizing with his gestures, his paralysis. Slipping into Kirchner's loose costume of neurosis, he tries it on, transforming himself. Soon after *'Heroes'* is finished, Bowie starts to paint more and more ambitious neo-Expressionist pictures, photographing them and mounting the prints in photo albums, *Berlin Landscape with J. O.* one of them from 1978 is called, referring to Jim Osterberg, alias Iggy Pop, in Tiergarten park. The picture gives an idea of how much the play of colour in Otto Mueller's *Lovers between Garden Walls* must have affected him, thin branches in front of a sky of pastel blue, a golden meadow, Iggy Pop's distorted facial features. All this is more an atmosphere than a scene, looking, though, like an imitation from an adult education art course of Jörg Immendorff, one of the best-known contemporary German painters. Bowie had shown his friend's head similarly deformed and emaciated as this two years before in the acrylic *Portrait of J. O.*, the picture being reproduced in the programme of Bowie's world tour of 1978, along with a caricature-like charcoal sketch of the *'Heroes'* cover. This, in fact, is what ends up on the admission tickets and posters.

In the search for themes not showing artists or referring to art, Bowie sees a little boy at the foot of the staircase to his apartment on Hauptstrasse. He paints him in oils, with a pale white face (the poor child apparently had toothache, Bowie argues later), surrounded by deep shadows, from where a bright handrail leads upstairs, getting brighter as it does. This *Child in Berlin* is still from 1977. *Turkish Father and Son* from the following year features

similarly bleak colours. Bowie is painting the troubled and the
afflicted during his time in Berlin. Most of it, as he himself is
aware, is only halfway to being good. His *Man with a Red Box*
from 1976 looks as though it has been copied from a Die Brücke
catalogue. The woodcut of a gigolo he is soon to use to advertise
his film *Just a Gigolo* is a study of Heckel's technique – a caricature,
not much more. In autumn 1977 Bowie meets up with Alan Yentob,
the director of *Cracked Actor*, in Cologne and tells him: 'I could
have been a painter. I wanted to be some kind of artist, I wanted
to prove myself in some field as an artist. And I didn't think I was
a very good painter so I went into music.'

Another time he says defiantly: 'I became a rock star. It's what
I do. It's not my whole life.' Bowie obviously feels he is not being
stretched, so in Berlin he straightaway gets involved with several
projects. This again is very typical of those who have come to live
in this city, that is, having a number of projects running in tandem,
contemporaneously. In Bowie's case these projects being: new
music of course, painting, in addition a book of short stories,
perhaps even directing in the near future, certainly more films.

Bowie apparently talked with Rainer Werner Fassbinder
about the possibility of adapting Brecht's *Threepenny Opera* for
the cinema. But nothing came of it. A similar case is the project
of making a film called *Wally* on the life of the painter Egon
Schiele directed by Clive Donner that was to be shot in Vienna
in July 1978 with Bowie in the main role alongside Charlotte
Rampling. It doesn't materialize. He turns down an offer by
the unpredictably extravagant Italian director Lina Wertmüller.

Instead, Bowie films in Berlin. With the film that comes about
in the spring of 1978 he reaches the goal of the dreams of his
youth. Once it has been made, Bowie leaves Berlin. He has now
achieved everything that there was to be achieved, 'A New Career
in a New Town', through the application of art and imagination.
For the reason that in this film Bowie can at last be in the Berlin

of the Twenties, even if only on celluloid – but his life is mainly made up of celluloid and photographic paper, isn't it? And that's where, against the backdrop of Weimar, he meets the greatest actress to come out of his favourite German films of the period. Bowie shares the screen with a woman who made the same journey as him 40 years before in the opposite direction, fleeing to Hollywood to get away from Hitler, never wanting to return to Berlin. Not once do the two of them meet in person, one of them filming in Berlin, the other in Paris. Okay, they only come together in the cutting-room, but even so, Bowie ends his time in Schöneberg making a film with the beautiful Marlene Dietrich from Schöneberg. The film is *Just a Gigolo*, called in German *Schöner Gigolo, armer Gigolo* ('Handsome Gigolo, Poor Gigolo') after the theme song.

Some time towards the end of 1977, as it happens, David Hemmings visits him in Blonay. The two of them have a lot in common, they get on like a house on fire. Just as Hemmings is the face of Britain in the Sixties, Bowie is the face of Britain in the Seventies. The director, who became world famous playing the photographer in Michelangelo Antonioni's *Blow-Up*, puts a

A scene from *Just a Gigolo*.

film project to Bowie. A Berlin story told via an old hit of the silent movie era. It's about a Prussian officer, returned from the First World War, with a weakness for the Nazis and for women, who at the end of the film gets a job as a gigolo before dying a hero's death in a street brawl, shot by his own people, who carry him to his grave under a flag with a swastika. He asks whether Bowie might be interested in such a story. There will be a few interesting actors taking part, Kim Novak, Maria Schell, Curd Jürgens – and then there's Marlene Dietrich.

Of course Bowie is interested, how could he be otherwise? 'Marlene Dietrich was dangled in front of me', he says later, when the film is finished, having been a flop, for a while nobody involved in Berlin wanting to look the other in the face. That's where the filming began in the middle of January 1978 with the crew consisting almost entirely of Germans, going on until the end of March. Bowie is financially involved with the film.

'Heroism is my destiny', is the first complete sentence he says in *Just a Gigolo*. The following one being 'Excuse me, I have a problem, I have to get back to Berlin.' The film plays with quotations from Bowie's career, exploiting Bowie's fame, even though Hemmings denies it. Likewise, it exploits the fame of all the other actors taking part, one-time Hollywood greats, but now reduced to acting bit parts in such eurotrash as this.

Instead of following the story, the viewer of it is more fascinated to watch Bowie parading in the company of these old pros. The plot is a bit weak in any case, Bowie playing the Prussian officer, Paul von Przygodski, who is seriously wounded approximately three minutes after the end of the war on the Western Front, lying in a field hospital in France for a long time before he can return home. Not to Berlin, even if the sets look like it, but to a Benny Hill film, the images speeding up all the time, accompanied by an out-of-tune piano, full of double entendres. It's a Benny Hill film all right that Marlene Dietrich is acting in. This is to be her last film role, the producer Rolf Thiele came especially to Paris to persuade her. Finally it is settled by $250,000 for two days' filming. For this fee *die Dietrich* portrays the madam to the Prussian military academy, she is Baroness von Semering and Bowie one of her callboys, a polished figure with the rank and the bearing of an officer.

Just a Gigolo heaps together so many clichés that it becomes almost a new genre in its own right. The film's version of the Twenties uses every hackneyed stereotype, including monocles and gay Nazi vegetarians. The widespread view that German troops had been stabbed in the back by the ruling powers in Germany at the end of the War. Proletarian cloth caps. Leather jackets. Sleazy hotels, dilettantes, and deposed princes keeping show girls, and in the midst of it all, Bowie playing Paul who has lost everything and is now selling himself as a gigolo to all the ladies of Berlin. He comes over as a robot. He can't even say 'Mutti' properly to his screen mother played by Maria Schell, 'Mooty!' is what he comes out with, 'Mooty!', making one wonder how he might have pronounced his aristocratic name. Fortunately he doesn't have to say 'Przygodski' too often. But after *Just a Gigolo* we can see why Antonia Maaß had to spend so long with Bowie getting him finally able to sing 'Heroes' in German.

Hemmings recuts the film twice, shortening it considerably in the process, after *Just a Gigolo* was badly received at the Cannes Film Festival in the summer of 1978. Nevertheless there are a few scenes that are worthy of note, a few jokes that are funny, such as Bowie at the start in an original black-and-white film clip walking around Anhalt station boasting, 'I'm coming close to my lifelong purpose', and when his first love, Cilly, played by Sydne Rome, asks what that is, he says, 'I don't know yet, but people are taking notice.' The film is an obvious spin-off of *Cabaret*, but it somehow fails to hit the spot, too shallow to be a political satire on the rise of the Nazis, not clever enough to be a comedy melodrama. A farce is all that *Just a Gigolo* is, and if it hadn't been for Dietrich, whose appearance is eagerly awaited right from the start, loudly heralded 'with pride' by the opening credits, the film would be almost totally without suspense. Finally we see Dietrich sitting in an easy chair, eyeing her latest acquisition in the form of Paul, who is intercut with the scene, and delivers her lines with just enough commitment to give the film a touch of authentic Berlin magnificence. Later she sings 'Just a Gigolo'. Her voice is still her voice, husky, knowing and emphatic. This is how she sounds a few years later in Maximilian Schell's famous documentary, a tape recording off the set. *That* is really her last great appearance on screen, not the one with Bowie in *Just a Gigolo*. In Paris Schell asks her why she doesn't want to appear in front of the camera any more, and Dietrich answers: 'I have been photographed to death', a fate shared by Bowie more and more during this period.

What was it like with Marlene Dietrich?, he is asked later on TV, a few days before the premiere of their film together, which took place on 16 November 1978 at the Gloria Filmpalast in Berlin, though Bowie doesn't go. 'I wish I knew', Bowie replies, 'I must ask somebody who worked with her.' In fact, she didn't come to the set in Berlin, however many times they begged her to. And then Bowie mentions that she went to America before the war and only ever came back once in peacetime, but she was treated as a traitor in her homeland and therefore decided never to set foot on German soil again. 'I stay in Paris, all the way through the film she said this', Bowie claims. 'And I quite agree with her. We talked to each other on the phone and we decided it would be fine if I did my bit in Berlin and she did hers in Paris.' He adds that this solution suited the film just fine, as 'she's forever the observer really', a mysterious wonderful Cocteau character. 'I wish I had met her a long time ago.'

That was before the premiere. And the way Bowie talks about his film here, slightly sceptically but still proud of it, sounds like a

promise. It's a promise that isn't kept, though. 'All my 32 Elvis
Presley movies rolled into one', Bowie says later, after the
premiere at the Berlin Gloria Palast. The reviews are scathing,
accusing Bowie now of not being able to act. In Germany the film
is not even shown in cinemas in the version cut for the premiere.
Just a Gigolo is nevertheless one of the high points of Bowie's
cinema career. It moves on from one costume drama to another,
from historical to fantasy subject matter. On screen as well Bowie
has on numerous occasions given his fans the feeling that they are
not living in the same period as their hero. Starting with *The Man
Who Fell to Earth*, his first feature film, he has aimed at avoiding
the present. Later Bowie plays Andy Warhol in Julian Schnabel's
Basquiat. He plays an ancient vampire in *The Hunger*; he plays
Nikola Tesla, the inventor of the alternating current, in *The
Prestige*. He plays Jareth, the Goblin King, in *Labyrinth*; he is
Pontius Pilate in Martin Scorsese's *The Last Temptation of Christ*;
he is a hardnosed businessman in the swinging Fifties of *Absolute
Beginners;* and a British soldier in a Japanese prisoner-of-war camp
in *Merry Christmas, Mr Lawrence*. On the rare occasions when
he acts in a contemporary film, as in the case of *Zoolander* or
Christiane F., he doesn't have a role but makes a cameo appearance.
In which case he is playing himself: David Bowie, Superstar. That
is his here and now.

   During the filming of *Just a Gigolo*, he is interviewed by a
journalist from *Rolling Stone*. It's the same one who witnessed
Bowie ordering his lunch in German. He says a few things about
Berlin to him that are critical and objective, he doesn't seem to be
dazzled by Speer's Cathedral of Light any more. One thing Bowie
says is that every older Berliner he meets tells him that he was a
Communist in the war and claims, 'But our family kept Jews in
ze attic' and 'zere was street fighting all the time in Berlin.' Before
he talks in this accent, he glances over his shoulder quickly, having
acquired the gesture familiar to Germans when suspecting that

they are being overheard. 'Which is true, that's why Hitler put his thumb on the city and decided to set up base here, because this was the most troublesome spot. There was always a very large Communist faction.' Hitler, always Hitler. Berlin, always Berlin.

> The rest of Germany can't stand Berliners, and Berliners look down on the rest of Germany. As far as they're concerned, they have a much stronger wit, very caustic, cynical wit. It's kind of like New York or London. Big city wit. They're very matter-of-fact about celebrities, music, trends, whatever. It makes it a very good place for someone like me to live, because I can be incredibly anonymous. You never get stopped here. They don't seem particularly joyful about seeing a famous face.

When Bowie talks about Marlene Dietrich on TV he sums up what else he has achieved recently during his time in Berlin. He says he has been trying to write a book of short stories. Perhaps he'll do a bit of directing in the near future, he'll certainly be appearing in more films, that's one thing he can say now for sure. On the other hand, he only wants to go on tour every two years. 'I want to be a good painter again', Bowie says. 'That's my really big dream.' He tells another journalist that he would like to apply to an art academy, either in Berlin or Basel. While finishing filming he produces some woodcuts. He calls himself a 'generalist', as that sounds better than jack-of-all-trades. He starts on a world tour, going from Europe to Australia. 'I need the money', he says bluntly. Adrian Belew, formerly with Frank Zappa, joins the band as a guitarist. Bowie says, 'The fine arts, generally, are my high seas – that's the course I take my ship on. Because one thing I would have adored to have been, more than anything else, is a real old-fashioned adventurer and discover new lands.'

That's just how his next album sounds, the last of the Berlin
Triptych, constantly on the move and full of yearning for faraway
places. *Lodger*, it's called. A lodger is what he is in Berlin, that's
also what most of the other people who have come to live in
the city remain. *'Ich habe noch einen Koffer in Berlin'*, 'I still have a
suitcase in Berlin', is what Ronald Reagan says at the Brandenburg
Gate in June 1987, and what he means is the usual, that he always
comes back to Berlin because he feels at home there. You can take
it a different way, though, the statement becoming emblematic of
Berlin as a place one is always passing through. This stopping-off
point where you stay but never properly unpack, uncertain
whether you have got to be moving on.

Work begins on *Lodger* in July 1978, soon after the filming
of *Just a Gigolo* has finished and after the first part of his world
tour. He assembles his team at the superb Mountain Studios in
Montreux, a total contrast to the pigeon loft that is Hansa Studios,
even though it soon gets terribly hot there with eight people in a
confined space. Some even claim they can make out the effect of
this high temperature in the ten new tracks. It's also caused by
friction, Eno and Bowie giving the studio musicians a hard time
with their rather arbitrary methods of creating an outstanding,
unorthodox and above all *different* rock music. Bowie insists on
the musicians swopping over their instruments. Andrew Belew
is not allowed to listen to the tracks he is to play guitar to. Eno
writes chords up on a board and points to them with a stick,
the musicians are supposed to follow him note by note. Bloody
professor, the band mutters. Stupid schoolboys, Eno replies.

But the famous Berlin air, *Berliner Luft*, is still missing. Not
just because *Lodger* is recorded in Montreux, a long way from the
Wall, and in the end the mixing is carried out at the Hit Factory
in New York, the Bowie–Eno collaboration having hit the buffers.
In the months before Montreux they hadn't seen much of one
another. They both have an idea, it's true, about how the new

album should sound, though not the same one. 'It started off extremely promising and quite revolutionary', Eno says, 'and it didn't seem to quite end that way.' They drift apart, like Ground Control and Major Tom, they are now on their way to different galaxies, Eno getting heavily into research on his ambient music and Bowie having sufficiently taken on board Eno's revolutionary ideas to make use of them in his superstar music. Not until the album *Outside* almost twenty years later do they get together again. 'I've learned some of Brian's methods quite thorougly', Bowie says in the summer of 1978, 'and I'm fairly competent with them, so I can utilize them on my own.' Apparently they argued a lot in the studio in Montreux. The pressure to come up with an equally brilliant third part of the Berlin Triptych was very great, at least that's what Bowie's guitarist Carlos Alomar claims. After this third part, Bowie and Eno go their separate ways, but they don't part in anger. They merely seem to be tired. The music they are producing collaboratively comes across as tired. Bowie and Eno don't need each other any more.

Lodger is a job to put together, and, however unique some of the tracks on it turned out, the album all in all sounds complacent and mannered through lack of direction. Bowie gets bogged down in too many ideas that are not thought through. Twice he recycles tunes that he used years before. His old hit 'All the Young Dudes' is played backwards, becoming 'Move On'; the last piece, 'Red Money', is purely and simply Iggy Pop's 'Sister Midnight' on *The Idiot* with new lyrics. 'Project Cancelled', Bowie sings in the chorus. Many of the biographers say that with this he has done a complete circle, that this is where the curtain comes down on the Berlin Triptych, 'Sister Midnight', the first track on *The Idiot*, having been the start of the very project that Bowie is now bringing to an end. He denies it on the grounds that the line was nothing more than a whim. Besides, he had always intended to use the term 'triptych', the three albums suiting him fine.

The album admittedly isn't as badly received as *Just a Gigolo*, but neither is anybody quite so enthusiastic about it as they were about *'Heroes'*, which prompted even John Lennon to write better music. Most of those reviewing *Lodger* sound rather irritated, with Jon Savage in *Melody Maker* clearly yawning aloud as he asks 'Will the Eighties really be this boring?' This is amusing, but then again a bit unfair, and above all it suggests a jaded palate. That's because one has in the meantime come to expect Bowie to be ahead of the curve on the big questions of the future. He can see into the future, at least so his label claims. And what can Bowie on *Lodger* see in his crystal ball? An end to hierarchies, ethnobeats and DJs. One number comes crashing onto the scene like Neu!, that's 'Red Sails'. The next track, 'Repetition', sounds like Talking Heads, on their *Fear of Music* album which comes out a year later, produced by Eno.

Lodger is a transitional album for Bowie. When the Seventies, his own decade, slowly draws to an end, he slips effortlessly into the role that he is to play in the world of pop right into the twenty-first century, turning into the great generalist of radical tendencies and innovations, the popularizer and guru. This change doesn't become obvious right away, because there is too much cool, new stuff mixed in with the imitations. The single 'Look Back in Anger' for instance has given rise to a number of doubles, for example 'Love Song' by Simple Minds and 'Love Like Blood' by Killing Joke. But the amount of eccentricity for others to take their cue from and build on starts to diminish on Bowie's albums. He himself is aware that he is slowly losing touch. As Bloch would put it, he is more and more in the same Now as other people, and he knows it. 'Well David, what shall I do?', he wonders using the third person on 'Teenage Wildlife' in 1980, a distant cousin of 'Heroes', giving as a clear answer: 'Don't ask me.' In general the need to establish his place in history gets stronger. On *Lodger* Bowie plays his own numbers backwards and also varies how they move forwards. Two years later he is to resurrect Major Tom – on the next album *Scary Monsters* in his hit 'Ashes to Ashes'.

On the day *Lodger* is launched, 18 May 1979, Bowie has long since left 155 Hauptstrasse. He probably moved out right after finishing the filming of *Just a Gigolo* at the end of February 1978. That's what is supposed to have happened anyway. You can't rightly say, though, as Bowie is after all hardly ever in Berlin any more but on tour, in TV studios, on vacation in Africa. Sometime during this period he moved into a loft in Manhattan, somewhere between Greenwich Village and Chelsea. He becomes a New York resident, has remained so to this day, though at that time keeping the house in Switzerland where his son is going to school. And he also has a flat in London. The tenancy agreement for Schöneberg is supposed to last until 1981, the year when Bowie returns to Hansa Studios to record Brecht's *Baal* with Tony Visconti, which became a television production. Iggy Pop stays on in Berlin in any case, out of love. He has had his own apartment for some time, in the back courtyard of 155 Hauptstrasse. At some point Bowie chucked him out because Iggy raided his fridge just once too often (for it was Bowie who actually did the shopping at KaDeWe).

The Berlin images gradually start to blur. In David Mallet's video for 'Look Back in Anger' Bowie is shown as a painter. He is standing in a garret looking at his portrait, removing the paint from the canvas, and everytime he removes it, it reappears on his face. This is one of his most powerful images, not just in Berlin: gaining so much from art that it reappears on his own body. Bowie's grotesquely dashed off portrait shows him with angel's wings. He is Walter Benjamin's famous angel of history irresistibly propelled into the future, his face turned towards the past.

And then Bowie finally also says goodbye to Romy Haag, at least that's how she takes it. In the video for 'Boys Keep Swinging', likewise made by Mallet, Bowie appears in drag three times – as

Lauren Bacall, Marlene Dietrich and Bet Lynch, the British soap opera character from TV's *Coronation Street*. Each time Bowie appears with make-up in women's clothes, tears his wig off, smudging the lipstick over his face, just like Romy does in her club, night after night, at the end of the show; it's a transvestite routine. The two of them break up because Bowie is upset at the way Romy has blabbed about their relationship in the Berlin papers, whatever form that relationship took. It's time to bring it to an end. Finally, in the shape of Bet Lynch, Bowie briefly puts his hand up to his lips in a farewell kiss, blown at the camera, Goodbye to Berlin. Goodbye, changing roles. Goodbye, make-up. Goodbye, all the glamour and razzmatazz of the so-called Golden Twenties.

But he still can't get away from using his body as a quotation. On the cover of *Lodger* Bowie is lying on his back with his body in a funny bent position and his face contorted; this posture is very reminiscent of the terrorist Andreas Baader when found dead in his cell on 18 October 1977. There is a photo to prove it, a myth being nothing if there isn't a photo. Bowie also reproduced a photo of the corpse of Che Guevara in the booklet on *Lodger*. *'Heroes'* comes out four days before that night at Stammheim prison. Without meaning to, this album becomes the soundtrack to that Autumn in Germany. At the same time Eno writes a song called 'R.A.F.'; Bowie doesn't go as far as this in his next album, though. He only tries on the costume, seeing clothes as stories, and sings about the Middle East, writing *Lodger* at the top, after the name of people of no fixed abode. He knows Rainer Werner Fassbinder but whether he also saw *Deutschland im Herbst* (*Germany in Autumn*), the German omnibus film of October 1977, a classic of the New German Cinema, in which Fassbinder appeared stark naked, we don't know. Anyone watching it, with Bowie's music in mind, will recognize certain images: A junkie who panics when he hears police sirens. Isolation. Paranoia. Gloomy apartments. A film project that sets out to refer back to the revolutionary films

of the Twenties. And Wolf Biermann, the singer-songwriter sings:
'*Was wird bloß aus unseren Träumen?* / *In diesem zerrissenen Land*'
('What is to become of our dreams? / In this divided land');
Biermann lost his homeland, stripped of his citizenship of the
GDR, on the same day as Bowie discovered a new one with *Low*.
This was exactly one year before that Autumn in Germany.

Every month since first arriving at Hansa Studios in August
1976, Bowie has been slowly starting to feel better. 'Berlin was
my clinic. It brought me back in touch with people', he says later.
'But I would still have days when things were moving round the
room even when I was sober. It took two years to cleanse my
system.' Two years during which Bowie changes until he thinks
he has arrived in the present. He reads daily newspapers, *The
Times* for example and the *International Herald Tribune*. He sets his
watch to Central European time. 'I honestly believe that what you
see now is myself', he says to Jean Rook of the *Daily Express* on
the day *Just a Gigolo* premieres. Even so he turns up that evening
on the red carpet in a kimono despite the fact that he has agreed
to dress in the style of the film. Bowie has been trying on different
costumes for some time, though. The period of proletarian cloth
caps is now over.

'Give us a shout when you think it's long enough', Eno is
supposed to have said when they were recording the instrumental
'Moss Garden' at Hansa, and Bowie looked at his watch and said,
'Yeah, that'll probably do.' He brings an end to his time in Berlin
in a similarly offhand way. At some moment or other time simply
ran out. 'Then Berlin was . . . over', he puts it bluntly. 'I had not
intended to leave Berlin, I just drifted away. Maybe I was getting
better. It was an irreplaceable, unmissable experience.' Berlin was
irreplaceable. Bowie, who knew how to tempt his musicians into
better performances using flattery, sends farewell presents, even
years later. He knows how much he owes to his myth. 'There's
an artistic tension in Berlin', he now says, 'that I've never come

across the like of anywhere else. Paris? Forget it. Berlin has it.'
He can't express how free he felt there. 'For the first time, the
tension was outside me rather than within me.' And on occasions
it sounds as though what Bowie says about Berlin had been
written for him by Ernst Bloch: 'It was either very young or very
old people. There were no family units in Berlin. It was a city of
extremes. It vacillated between the absurd – the whole drag,
transvestite night-club type of thing – and real radical marxist
political thought.'

In the last months before he leaves 155 Hauptstrasse for good,
Bowie is basically on the road the whole time. He takes Zowie
with him on safari in Kenya. The boy is now called Joey, perhaps
because he also needed bringing down to earth. *Stage* is released
after the never-ending world tour of 1978; it's a live album on
which, the story goes, Tony Visconti has to remove the booing
during 'Sense of Doubt'. And as 1979 is drawing to an end and
Bowie is still doing promotion for *Lodger*, the peculiar final Berlin
album that doesn't have much to do with Berlin any more, he is
at last given a theatrical role as well. This time, in America. *The
Elephant Man*, with performances in Denver, Chicago and New
York, is his first real success on the stage. The critics go wild,
Bowie playing John Merrick, the Victorian circus monster, the
deformed outsider with artistic tendencies. Another historical
figure, another metamorphosis, another freak, amiable yet
misunderstood, who is destroyed by being dragged into the
limelight and stared at.

There is no parting scene, no stage direction, no last gasp, the
curtain falls undramatically. David Bowie leaves Berlin just as he
came, simply moving on. Moving on from one role to the next.

CODA: WHERE IS HE NOW?

He took his apartment keys away with him. But now they are hanging there once more, exhibited behind the glass: two fairly large keys, typical of the ones used for the wooden doors of Berlin *altbau* buildings, and four shorter ones with rubberized handles. Next to them there is a timetable for the Berlin public transport system. And the lyrics of 'Heroes' handwritten on squared paper. And a postcard without a date: 'Dear David', it says, 'it would be great if we could see you again before we go. Christopher Isherwood.'

More than 35 years have gone by since Bowie left Berlin. And in the spring of 2014 he returns in style, with a giant retrospective dedicated to his lifetime achievements on display at the Martin-Gropius Bau, a stone's throw from Hansa Studios. 'David Bowie Is' has already been shown in his home city, London, at the Victoria & Albert Museum the year before, at last declaring him a Gesamtkunstwerk, a total work of art in his own right. It brings together 300 exhibits from Bowie's enormous private archive, costumes, storyboards for films, letters, song lyrics, photos, illustrations. His copies of Eno's 'Oblique Strategy Cards', the corners of the cards well worn, are also on display. Letters he sent to Marlene Dietrich (and got from her) while shooting *Just a Gigolo*. A photo of him and Coco Schwab in East Berlin and another one showing the kitchen table at 155 Hauptstrasse. A self-portrait from 1978 hangs on the wall in the style of the *'Heroes'*

cover, and some of the other paintings he did in Berlin, his portrait of Yukio Mishima, and Iggy in the Tiergarten. Along with the timetable for the BVG, the Berlin public transport system, a postcard from Isherwood and the keys to 155 Hauptstrasse.

In fact, as the tenant of a Berlin apartment you don't get your deposit back if you keep your keys. Either it is terribly conventional to expect such rules to apply to someone like Bowie. Or he is still resident there, in theory at least.

No, David Bowie has of course been living in New York for some time. For years he led a rather secluded life there, hardly ever appearing in public, not releasing music any more – until suddenly on the day of his 66th birthday, 8 January 2013, he reappeared as if from nowhere bearing a new song and a video.

'Where Are We Now?' the new song is entitled. A solemn drumbeat, a guitar in the background only now and then setting the tone until towards the end it comes to life with a vengeance. In Bowie's songbook you could classify the song somewhere between 'Teenage Wildlife' (on *Scary Monsters*) and 'Strangers When We Meet' (on *Outside*), only much, much slower, elegiac, wiser. Against this lazy rhythm and sparing notes on the guitar we hear Bowie singing with a cracked voice, singing about Berlin.

And he is speaking in German again. Or at least a few German words: Postsdamer Platz. Bösebrücke. Dschungel. Nürnberger Strasse. KaDeWe. And still Bowie has trouble getting his mouth round the words, just like before, when Antonia Maaß tried to straighten out his pronunciation of the German translation of 'Heroes' so that he could sing it passably well.

So many artists after him have paid homage to Bowie's time in Berlin. Now he is doing it himself. No end of TV cameras have stood in front of 155 Hauptstrasse. Now you can see the building in the video for 'Where Are We Now?' made by the installation

Bowie at home in Berlin.

artist Tony Oursler. The song is a unique act of establishing one's place in history. Nothing new for Bowie, in fact. He has always been doing something of the kind, but this time he is doing it without any trace of irony. Without disguise. Without double meaning. Not like in the case of Major Tom, who Bowie said was a junkie; not like in the case of Ziggy Stardust, who he murdered on stage. But Major Tom and Ziggy Stardust were just characters that he had at some time made up and then wanted to get rid of as they had got too close to him or were becoming a burden. This time it goes deeper. 'Sitting in the Dschungel', Bowie sings, 'on Nürnberger Strasse. A man lost in time near KaDeWe.'

Here then is somebody caught in a time loop. He is returning to the scenes of his three happy years: *The Potsdamer Platz where I recorded the most groundbreaking music of my life; the 'Dschungel' where I danced; KaDeWe, where on the sixth floor I bought groceries that Iggy helped himself to.*

If 'Where Are We Now?' were not such a damn good song, one might perhaps accuse Bowie of going off on a nostalgia kick in a desperate attempt to regain his lost youth. But the song rises above all such sentimentality. And it shows beyond all misunderstanding that David Bowie is more keenly aware than all his fans and critics how significant *Low* and *'Heroes'* were for his career.

For his return to the world after ten years, instead of one single new song, Bowie could also have revived others from his cast of characters. That's exactly what he did in the video for his next new single. In 'The Stars (Are Out Tonight)' we see his doubles, a young Bowie from the *Hunky Dory* phase for example, and even the limo from *The Man Who Fell to Earth* comes back into view.

But first of all David Bowie returns to the ghosts of Berlin. 'Just walking the dead', he sings over and over again in 'Where Are We Now?' And in doing so he himself solves the riddle of his time at 155 Hauptstrasse. Because this is exactly what he did in Berlin: he went for a short walk with the dead, with Ernst Ludwig Kirchner and Erich Heckel, with Brecht, and with Marlene Dietrich, who after all only appeared to him as a ghost when he was filming *Just a Gigolo*, with her in Paris, him in Berlin. Then Bowie continued on his walk, to New York, into the '80s with *Let's Dance* and the drum 'n' bass of the '90s and on into the twenty-first century, falling silent at some point, and now here he is, returning to Berlin, but very much to the ghosts of his own past.

These he embraces, but at the same time, contemporaneously, he keeps them at a distance, the cover of *The Next Day*, the new album, released in March 2013, is the one from *'Heroes'*, but at one remove and with something stuck on the top. It has a white square applied to the spot where Bowie in 1977 imitated Ernst Ludwig Kirchner's frozen facial expression as Erich Heckel painted him in 1917. Only Bowie's hands stick out from under the sticker. The title is erased. In 1977 he had just put the word *'Heroes'* in quotation marks. Now he has totally obliterated it.

Walter Benjamin's angel of history was propelled into the future to which his back was turned, staring at the wreckage of the past. The experiment with time set in train by David Bowie at 155 Hauptstrasse, having itself now become a part of history, is dawning on the next day. Bowie himself has placed the key to his work right in front of our noses. All we have to do is take it down off the hook and there we are, in Berlin.

SOURCES AND BACKGROUND

Over the years I have gathered information and ideas for this book from various biographies and biographical essays on Bowie. Many of the quotations from him and his contemporaries used here are to be found in the following books.

David Buckley, *David Bowie: The Complete Guide to his Music* (London, 2004)

Peter and Leni Gillman, *Alias David Bowie* (London, 1986)

Heinz Rudolf Kunze, *David Bowie: Der Favorit oder: Die vielen Gesichter im leeren Spiegel* (in Idole 8, Treffpunkt im Nirgendwo, herausgegeben von Siegfried Schmidt-Joos, Ullstein, 1986)

Barry Miles et al., *David Bowie Black Book: The Illustrated Biography* (London, 1981)

Christopher Sandford, *David Bowie: Loving the Alien* (London, 1996)

Thomas Jerome Seabrook, *Bowie in Berlin: A New Career in a New Town* (London, 2008)

Nick Stevenson, *David Bowie: Fame, Sound and Vision* (Cambridge, 2006)

George Tremlett, *David Bowie: Living on the Brink* (New York, 1997)

Shelton Waldrep, *The Aesthetics of Self-Invention: Oscar Wilde to David Bowie* (Minneapolis, MN, 2004)

Chris Welch, *David Bowie: We Could Be Heroes: The Stories Behind Every David Bowie Song* (New York, 1999)

Hugo Wilcken, *Low* (New York and London, 2005)

I have used the following autobiographies and biographies by Bowie's friends
and contemporaries:

Angela Bowie, *Free Spirit* (London, 1981)

——, with Patrick Carr, *Backstage Passes: Life on the Wild Side with David Bowie*
(London, 1993)

Christiane F., *Wir Kinder vom Bahnhof Zoo* (Düsseldorf, 1993), trans. as '*H*':
Autobiography of a Child Prostitute and Heroin Addict (London, 1981)

Romy Haag, *Eine Frau und mehr,* unter Mitarbeit von Martin Schacht
(Chesham, 1999)

Paul Stump, *Unknown Pleasures: Roxy Music, a Cultural Biography* (New York,
1998)

Eric Tamm, *Brian Eno: His Music and the Vertical Sound of Color* (New York,
1995)

Jürgen Teipel, *Verschwende deine Jugend* (Berlin, 2001)

Paul Trynka, *Iggy Pop* (Berlin, 2008)

Tony Visconti, *Bowie, Bolan and the Brooklyn Boy: The Autobiography* (London,
2007)

For sketching in the context of Bowie's time in the Hauptstrasse and the picture
of Berlin in general, the following were invaluable:

Timothy Garton Ash, *The File: A Personal History* (London, 1997)

Ernst Bloch, *Erbschaft dieser Zeit* (Berlin, 1985), trans. as *Heritage of Our Times,*
by Neville and Stephen Plaice (London, 1991)

Max Frisch, *Montauk* (Berlin, 1978)

——, *Montauk,* trans. Geoffrey Skelton (New York, 1976)

Christopher Isherwood, *Goodbye to Berlin* (London, 2001)

Olaf Leitner, *West-Berlin! Westberlin! Berlin (West)! Die Kultur – die Szene – die
Politik. Erinnerungen an eine Teilstadt der 70er und 80er Jahre* (Berlin, 2002)
[contains the radio discussion between Edgar Froese und Olaf Leitner]

Rory MacLean, *Berlin: Imagine a City* (London, 2014)

Wolf Jobst Siedler and Elisabeth Niggemeyer, *Die gemordete Stadt. Abgesang
auf Putte und Straße, Platz und Baum* (Munich, 1993)

The important journals for me included:

> Du, vol. 741: *David Bowie. Beruf: Popstar* [contains the interview between
> Hanif Kureishi and Bowie]
> *Mojo Classic*, special edition: *60 Years of David Bowie* (January 2007)
> *Playboy* [Germany], vol. 1 (1978) [contains the Bowie interview and Michel
> Foucault]
> *Rolling Stone* [Germany], vol. 10 (1997) [contains a special section on *Bowie*
> *in Berlin*]

Filmed material that helped me during my research included Alan Yentob's
documentary *Cracked Actor* as well as the short *The Image* (1967) and Lindsay
Kemp's play *Pierrot in Turquoise*, and of course the videos for Bowie's songs in
the 'Berlin Triptych'. Also useful was the DVD *David Bowie Under Review, 1976–1979:
The Berlin Trilogy* (in-akustik 2006), containing the film material, videos and
particularly comments by British music critics such as Mark Prendergast.
The film *Schöner Gigolo, armer Gigolo* is available on DVD in the German version
and in English as *Just a Gigolo* (Kinowelt 2005). The DVD of *The Man Who Fell
to Earth* with a wealth of extra material is available in the UK (Optimum 2007).
Both *Cabaret* and *Christiane F. – Wir Kinder vom Bahnhof Zoo* (*Christiane F. – We
Children from Bahnhof Zoo*) are on DVD (both Euro Video).

Thilo Schmied's 'Music-Tours Berlin' take you behind the scenes at the Hansa
Studios and to the Hauptstrasse.

An invaluable source of information about Bowie in the '70s can be found at
www.bowiegoldenyears.com, in which in addition to a chronology Roger Griffin
provides a large collection of articles from newspapers and magazines.

The internal report by the Stasi about the events surrounding the Bowie
concert on 6 June 1987 are to be found in the archive of the office of the
Federal Commissioner for the Records of the State Security Service of the
former GDR (Der Bundesbeauftragte für die Unterlagen des Staatssicherheits-
dienstes der ehemaligen Deutschen Demokratischen Republik, usually referred
to as Der Bundesbeauftragte für die Stasi-Unterlagen and abbreviated BStU)
under MfS-ZOS 3769.

For the sections on crisis rhetoric in Britain in the 1970s I am indebted to research
undertaken by the contemporary historian Dominik Geppert.

And, finally, I obtained a lot of information on the Die Brücke artists and their works from the descriptive index *Brücke-Museum Berlin. Malerei und Plastik*, ed. Magdalena M. Moeller (Munich, 2006).

ACKNOWLEDGEMENTS

Thanks to Antonia Maaß, Eduard Meyer, Dr Cord Riechelmann, Michael Rother, Stephan Vogdt, Dr Dominik Geppert, Matthias Liese / BStU, Dietmar Dath, the friends in my Berlin and Frankfurt editorial offices, Anke Göbel, Dr Henning Ritter, Florian Illies, Professor Richard Langston, Professor Sarah McGaughey, but above all to Bobby (*Tramps like us*) and most of all to Melanie (*Baby, we were born to run*).

PHOTO ACKNOWLEDGEMENTS

Archiv Hansa Tonstudio: p. 74; Corbis: p. 168 (Christian Simonpietri / Sygma); DPA Picture Alliance: p. 6; Getty Images: p. 132 (Michael Ochs Archive); Andrew Kent: pp. 46, 49, 82, 89; Eduard Meyer: pp. 68, 143; Nachlass Erich Heckel, Hemmenhofen: p. 111; Christian Thiel: p. 62; Ullsteinbild: p. 70; Verwertungsgesellschaft BILD-KUNST: p. 138.

INDEX